This book is dedicated to my beautiful and always supportive wife, Lia, and my two daughters, Isabella and Nadia. It is also dedicated to every person I've worked with in my career, each having a lasting impact on my personal and professional life.

Table of Contents

→ # Million Dollar Journey

How to Launch a Seven-Figure Business

Erik J. Olson

Million Dollar Journey
How to launch a seven-figure business

Copyright 2021 Erik J. Olson

All rights reserved. No portion of this book may be reproduced, stored in a retrieval system, or transmitted in any form or by any means—electronic, mechanical, photocopy, recording, scanning, or other—except for brief quotations in critical reviews or articles, without the prior written permission from the author.

Printed in the United States of America

First Edition
ISBN: 979-8-5776828-6-6

The Valley of Death illustration is reprinted with permission of Verne Harnish from Scaling Up, page 25, copyright 2014.

Art Direction: Scott Massey
www.nohawk.com

Editor: Jennifer Jas
www.wordswithjas.com

00	Introduction	vii
01	The painted picture	001
02	Surveying the road ahead	007
03	Paving the entrepreneurial path	017
04	Taking your first steps on the path to $1M	031
05	Branding	045
06	Open for business	059
07	Getting clients	075
08	Getting paid	097
09	Managing the money	129
10	Hiring and firing	153
11	Developing your people	167
12	Goal-setting	189
13	Pivoting	201
14	The journey to $100 million	217
	About the author	227
	Array Mentors	229
	Acknowledgments	233
	Take notes	235

Introduction

→ Who *Million Dollar Journey* is for

Million Dollar Journey is for entrepreneurs and business owners who want to grow a million dollar business. Whether your business is established or brand new—or you haven't figured out what your business will be—this book is for you. If you have ambitions to grow a business and scale it to $1 million per year in revenue, then *Million Dollar Journey* will show you the way.

→ What you'll get out of this book

The freedom, fulfillment, and potential to make real money are part of the entrepreneurial spirit. But those ideals only matter when you actually start your business, and especially when you get to a point where your business is sustaining itself.

Starting a business is hard but will become easier once you understand and apply certain principles that you can learn and even master.

I'm going to step you through the most important aspects of starting and running a business. My goal is to lay out the most valuable components—the lessons I learned, and yes, even my biggest mistakes—that helped me grow the company to $1 million, so you can quickly apply them to grow your business.

Did you know that only 4 percent of businesses reach the $1 million mark? That means that 96 percent of businesses struggle forever, or die trying to reach the mark. I want you to join the 4 percent club of entrepreneurs who have reached the $1 million mark.

You will likely take a different route than I did on your million dollar journey. Our levels of education, experience, and skill sets are different, and our businesses are probably completely different in nature. But what I've found from talking with thousands of entrepreneurs in person and online is that we all seem to learn the same types of lessons along the way. And as business owners, we all seem to make similar mistakes.

Imagine if you held in your hands a map of the lessons to be learned and the mistakes to avoid before you started on your entrepreneurial journey. Maps make journeys easier. You know what direction you're heading in, you know your destination, you can predict the obstacles that'll be in your way, and you can reroute around them.

Million Dollar Journey is your map to getting to the $1 million mark—the 4 percent club—and to a more fulfilled and rewarding life than you're likely experiencing now. You will learn what I did right and, more importantly, what I did wrong. Learn from my mistakes instead of making them yourself, and you'll get your business up and running faster and easier than I did.

Let's be clear—I am not offering an overnight success program.

This will take much more time and much more effort than you've ever imagined. As Theodore Roosevelt said, "Nothing in this world is worth having or worth doing unless it means effort, pain, difficulty."

Achieving $1 million and beyond in revenue is definitely worth the effort. Now let's minimize the pain and difficulty.

→ 01

The painted picture

01 THE PAINTED PICTURE

It's a huge room.

We've planned this event for months. Years, really.

We're in Las Vegas, far from home, and I've flown out here several times recently for the final preparations.

By this point I know the room well. The party coordinator had shown me how the room would be laid out, what the decorations would look like, and where the tables and the stage would be placed. I'd visualized this room and the upcoming evening hundreds of times in my head. Tonight will be a special night for me and my company.

We always hold our company holiday party on the first Saturday in December, and this year is no exception. It's December 7th, but this year is an extra special event. I've been here for days preparing for this, but even after all that preparation, years of preparation, in fact, I'm a little late to the party.

As usual, it takes my wife, Lia, and me a bit longer to get ready for the party than we expected. Okay, it's really my beautiful wife who couldn't decide which shoes to pick. This is just as much a celebration of what we've been through as it is for what the company has achieved.

The elevator doors open and I can hear the roar of the band. It's early in the evening but the party is already in full swing.

Although there are plenty of bars in the ballroom, two more are outside in the hallway leading to the room. People are walking in and out of the ballroom. Some are going to the bar to get drinks, some are walking back in with drinks, and others are lingering in the large hall.

People are milling about everywhere. As we walk from the elevator to the ballroom entrance, people are warm and welcoming. Some stop and hug us, others shake our hands and congratulate us, and still others give us high-fives as we walk by.

It takes us a good twenty minutes before we enter the ballroom. This is the first time I've seen it filled with all our guests—all 472 employees and their significant others, plus several important clients, trusted advisors, and other VIPs. In all, we have about a thousand people in attendance.

To accommodate such a big party, we've laid out 140 tables that'll seat eight people each. The tables surround a giant dance floor in the front and center of the ballroom, and the dance floor has lights above and below it. Both sets of lights pulsate with the beat and change colors frequently. I notice a few disco balls reflecting light throughout the room at different times.

A series of fifteen-foot-tall monitors stretch across the front of the room from side to side. This won't be my largest audience, but this will be the most important.

The room is abuzz with activity. The celebration is just getting fired up. The four bars in the corners of the room are packed with bartenders and guests. Between the bartenders mixing up drinks, the cocktail waiters and waitresses bringing drinks to tables, and the staff walking around with platters of hors d'oeuvres, I estimate at least two hundred staffers on hand for the event.

The Roots, a popular hip-hop band from *The Tonight Show*, are wailing in the front of the dance floor. The dance floor is packed, the music is pumping, and the lights are throbbing.

A cocktail waitress offers us glasses of champagne. We accept, look at each other to cheers, and I see that she's all smiles. A big smile, wide eyes, and a little bit teary-eyed. As am I.

We clink glasses and kiss each other as usual. But this time, I hear cameras coming to life as two photographers capture the moment from different angles. It's been an incredible journey, full of highs and lows, and we couldn't have done it without each other's support.

My business partner and Array Digital co-founder, Kevin Daisey, is coming toward us. He arrived a bit early, and he's in a festive mood. He gives us both hugs. He's so excited. He's taken great risks along the way, and we've worked through difficult situations together over the past thirteen years since merging companies in 2017. All that effort meant that we achieved the goal we set for ourselves long ago—the goal that led up to this celebration.

The band has finished the last song in their set and out comes our emcee for the night, my good friend Zack Miller. As the band members leave the elevated stage in front of the dance floor, Zack takes over. His job right now is to transition from the first part of the night—music and dancing—to "the talk." Zack, always the performer, gets to work. He's whipping up the crowd, complimenting the band, and complimenting all the good-looking people at the black-tie affair laid out in front of him.

My wife and I are at the back of the dance floor, maybe fifty feet away from the stage. Zack is in full introduction mode, and I realize the moment I've been thinking about for the past decade is about to happen. He introduces me and invites me to the stage.

So many people are in the room. Many I know well, but several are new employees who I haven't had a chance to meet yet. It's a somewhat odd feeling when your employee knows you, but you don't know them yet. And nearly half of the people are my employees' guests, many of whom I've never seen before.

The company has grown so fast in the past few years that it's been practically impossible to visit each office on a regular basis to meet everyone. I want to be able to meet privately with each employee at least once a year, but the logistics make it difficult.

After shaking many hands and giving many hugs, I reach the stage. Zack is still there, mic in hand. He gives me a big bear hug, picking me up off my feet in the process, then hands me the microphone.

I grip it tight and give a roar into it. A big old, "Whoa ... we made it. Welcome to Las Vegas, baby!"

As the clapping subsides, I begin to pace the stage like I normally do when I give talks. Pacing gives me comfort and the ability to look at everyone straight in the eye. I try to speak as if I'm having a one-on-one conversation, but at scale. The more people I can connect with visually, and the more sets of eyes I lock in with, the more comfortable I feel.

I begin to retell the story. It's a story I've told many times before, the beginning of which I'm about to tell you in *Million Dollar Journey*.

The story is about how we finally achieved our company vision which we established way back in 2017. That vision—to grow into a $100-million-a-year digital marketing powerhouse—took us thirteen years to achieve, but we finally made it!

→ MILLION DOLLAR JOURNEY

Surveying the road ahead

What I described in the first chapter is referred to as the Painted Picture.

It's a vision of a future scene that has not yet happened. In this case, it's my vision of our 2030 holiday party after reaching $100 million in revenue.

A Painted Picture is conveyed in either present or past tense. Most people think of the future as a fuzzy concept of what may happen. The Painted Picture flips the concept around so you envision, in great detail, a future event as if it's happening now or already happened.

My whole career I've heard people ask, and I've asked, *What does success look like?* The answer is typically vague and not completely thought out. And that's how the Painted Picture is different. It's extremely visual. The Painted Picture injects you directly into a future scene so you can see it, feel it, hear it, smell it, and experience it.

Did you notice the level of detail in my Painted Picture? The event will be held on December 7, 2030. It's an out-of-town party in Las Vegas. I know how many people will be in attendance, how the room is laid out, who the band is, who the emcee is, who will be with me, and exactly how the night unfolds.

Different people have different ways of envisioning success. I've picked a long-term goal of $100 million in revenue. Others may be happy that their lifestyle business allows them to pay the bills so they can focus more on fun and family than on working. To each their own—you define your success.

I was first introduced to the concept of the Painted Picture in Brian Scudamore's book *Willing to Fail*. At the time, I hadn't yet met Brian, but we were both in the Entrepreneurs' Organization—EO for short—an entrepreneurial mastermind that has been integral to my journey. Brian had just published his book, and he selected several EO members to send it to.

What a surprise when the book showed up at my office with a letter from Brian. I didn't even know that the CEO of 1-800-GOT-JUNK was a member of EO. More CEOs like him would have an impact on me later in my story.

His book described his Painted Picture, which included launching 1-800-GOT-JUNK in thirty metropolitan areas, becoming the FedEx of junk removal, and getting on the Oprah Winfrey Show.

The book instantly gave me direction on how to describe my own Painted Picture. I felt so energized by his concepts that I posted the following in a review of his book in December 2018 ...

> If you don't already have a vision for your business, you need one. You have to know where you're heading or you may never get there. The Painted Picture concept takes it one step further. Tell the story of where you will be from the perspective of having already achieved the goal.
>
> As an example, my vision is to be a $100M company by 2030. That's great and all, but a more powerful way to communicate that vision would be to describe the company as if it were 2030, maybe at the holiday party. E.g.: "After 11 years of hard work, we now have offices in five large markets in the US, employ X number of creatives, and have earned $100M this year." That's the Painted Picture.

In retrospect, I'd heard of the concept before reading his book, but never by the name Painted Picture.

When I received Brian's book, I was in the midst of binging on business podcasts. One of my favorite podcasts at the time was the *MFCEO Project* hosted by Andy Frisella. In many episodes, Andy recounted how, during his early days in business when he was struggling to get his young company up and running, he began to envision his future success.

Andy doesn't refer to his vision of future success as a Painted Picture, but it is. My Painted Picture comes to life as a party to celebrate reaching $100 million in sales. He defined his vision of success quite differently.

He envisioned his future success in material terms. In particular, he imagined driving up to his private plane in his white Lamborghini, what the steering wheel felt like as he drove up, how he'd park and hear the Lambo's door as it opened above him, and how he'd step out and walk to the private plane waiting for him. As he grabbed the metal handrail on the plane's stairway, he could feel the cold steel tubing in his hand while climbing into the plane.

Now that's a vision of the future!

→ The first million really is the hardest

You've likely heard the phrase, *The first million is the hardest*. While it is true, it doesn't fully explain why it's hard at first and why it's easier after that.

Consider this: At some point in my business, I stopped incessantly worrying about whether the business would succeed or fail. The operations of the business got a little easier because I had the right amount of staff to take on the work. And new business opportunities greatly exceeded the natural decay of clients that occurs in just about any business.

That all happened shortly after crossing the threshold of $1 million in revenue per year.

Although it's just a number, and there's nothing magical about any number, this number does seem to be special. Once our company was generating $1 million in revenue consistently, everything seemed to suddenly snap into place. Everything got a little bit easier. That continued for another roughly $250,000 in annual revenue.

And then, what seemed like suddenly, things started to get hard again as we encountered new problems. But we enjoyed a plateau—a sweet spot—between $1 million and $1.25 million when things were just clicking, and we could do no wrong.

That sweet spot is what I want you to aim for. At least initially. Get there, and you have a viable business model. You've validated your idea. You offer a product or service that people are buying, and you've figured out how to sell and provide it.

Of course, you need to account for other details such as profit margins, long-term sustainability, competition, and market conditions, but once you've achieved your million dollar journey, you'll have accomplished something special. You'll have built a company that's proven a point. And the point is: You produce an offering that people want. You have a legitimate business and a viable future.

It's a significant enough obstacle that few companies ever reach the milestone. The majority of business owners walk away from their venture, or stop trying, well before achieving this milestone.

I can understand why. In the early days of my million dollar journey, I struggled so much that it was hard to see beyond any given project. I had no clue what next week would hold, never mind how the next decade or two would unfold.

Those early days, when you're first getting started and scrambling for revenue, are the most frightening.

→ The path to success

At the last company I worked for as an employee, the HR manager remarked on more than one occasion that the owner of the business was just like me and him, but was a few spots ahead of us. He used the analogy of people waiting in line to get into the movies and that the owner of the company simply got in line before we did.

It was a simplistic view of the business world. His premise was that lines move, and we'll all eventually get to where the owner was in his life if we just wait long enough.

I now realize that his view reduced the owner's hustle, grit, and determination down to mere luck and timing. As a naive younger version of myself, I assumed the business owner simply got lucky. He was in the right place at the right time and dumb luck turned him into a successful businessman. The HR manager's view reinforced that belief.

But now, knowing what I know about entrepreneurship and looking back at the difficulty and length of my million dollar journey, I recognize that the owner's success was not due to luck. It was not due to waiting in line longer than others. It was due to working hard, taking risks, and injecting smarts into the business.

The owner often showed us the company's growth charts over time and how they'd gone through good times and bad times. I experienced both in the five years I worked there.

The boom times were great—new contracts, new clients, new exciting projects, and lots of activity. But the slow times weren't quite as fun—canceled projects, rounds of layoffs, and "right-sizing." Their business adjusted, rightfully so.

That's not luck, and it's not just timing. That's strategy, that's experience, and that's being a good entrepreneur.

An entrepreneur's path to success is not a straight line. If you chart your progress over time, you'll see the ups and downs and zigs and zags all along the way.

You will be challenged. Your "perfect plans" will be tested. You will fail along the way. You must not only be prepared for these tests, but you must determine to persevere through the inevitable downtimes that come along with success. You must keep your future prize in mind.

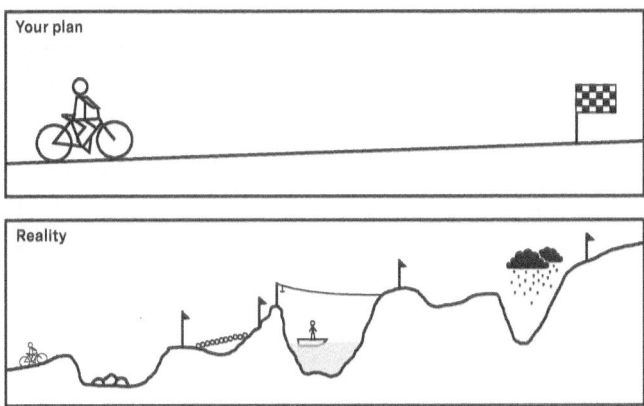

This image accurately portrays the journey with its inevitable ups, downs, and failures along the way. Source: George Couros

→ The valley of death

I hope you're already realizing that your journey will include a mix of great times on the peaks with your head in the clouds, as well as tough times in the pits with the walls closing in. During tough times, you put it all on the line to get to the next milestone, or you entrench and stay where you're at.

The first few years of my business were marked by significant growth. Once we broke the million dollar mark, our revenue mysteriously plateaued, then dropped a bit. Not because of a recession or an outside force, but because we started making mistakes.

The quality of our work decreased, and we weren't communicating as well internally or with clients. It seemed like every time I turned around, something was broken. Frustrated and not understanding the source of the problems, I tackled each issue individually and questioned everything.

To break out of our funk, we improved our processes, aligned better with our clients' needs, and formalized our marketing strategy. Things started to snap into place for us. Within a year, we were back above the $1 million mark and have continued to grow since then.

The book *Scaling Up* by Verne Harnish highlights just how hard it is for companies to grow. Verne identifies several substantial revenue milestones in a company's journey. Of the roughly twenty-eight million companies in the US at the time his book was published, only 4 percent made it to generating $1 million in revenue per year. As I mentioned in the Introduction, that means an astounding 96 percent either forever linger trying to break that threshold or die trying.

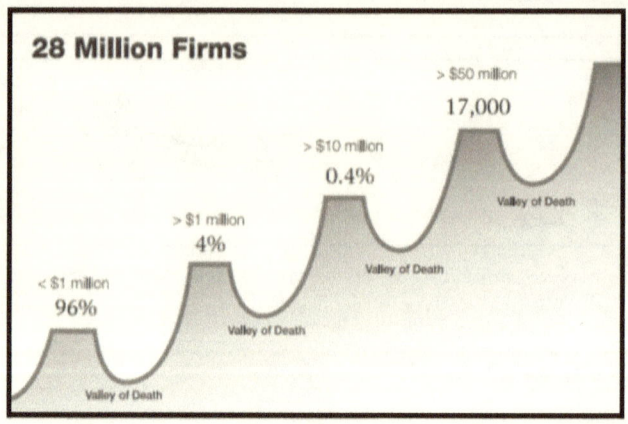

Source: *Scaling Up*

As revenue increases, the chances of reaching new milestones decrease substantially. Only seventeen thousand companies reach $50 million/year. That's only 0.06 percent of companies! Clearly, the chances of making it big are low. Very low. In *Scaling Up*, he portrays the journey punctuated by valleys of death.

In between each significant revenue milestone, there's a danger zone—a valley of death—that each company must get through in order to reach the next milestone. If you're not prepared for growth and you fall unknowingly into a valley of death, you may not emerge on the other side.

As you grow your company to reach the next milestone, your processes and people will need to change in order to get you there. You've probably heard the wise adage, "What got you here won't get you to where you're going."

You will encounter valleys of death in your journey too. Regardless of whether you are about to start your journey or you're well on your way, you can anticipate those valleys off in the distance. You can even plan ahead for them.

Million Dollar Journey prepares you with specific, actionable steps to climb out of the valleys and back up to the top of a peak. Another gorgeous vista awaits.

Chapter takeaways

1. A Painted Picture is your vivid vision of what your future success looks like. What does success look like for you?
2. The path to success is not a straight line. It will zig and zag and have ups and downs. Hang on ... it's going to be a wild ride!
3. As you grow, you'll encounter plateaus and valleys of death. To proceed on your journey, prepare for bad times when times are good.
4. Growth requires change, and change involves risk. If you want to grow, accept the risk.

Paving the
entrepreneurial path

It's a common belief that if the risk is large, the reward will be too. Entrepreneurs, like you and like me, believe the risk is worth taking. We dream about the possibility of success. Yet many are unprepared for the risks. And oh, many risks exist.

Entrepreneurship is a tough career choice. It can be risky, stressful, and challenging. Especially in the beginning. It doesn't even remotely resemble the safety of a nine-to-five in a cushy corporate cubicle, attending pointless meetings, taking long lunches, and cruising through the day until the mass exodus out the door a few minutes before 5 p.m.

Many entrepreneurs put in long hours, tons of energy, and loads of time as they struggle to get their company off the ground, to get the attention of prospective customers, and to survive the valley of death. More entrepreneurs struggle and fail than succeed. With the chance of success and riches being so slim, why do entrepreneurs start down such a precarious path?

For most of us, we kind of fall into it when we start a side gig to fill a need or fulfill a passion. Once it starts to grow, we see the possibilities of becoming a legit business owner.

You may not have realized it at the time, but you likely encountered opportunities in your formative years that propelled you into thinking like an entrepreneur. Looking back, you'll likely see patterns emerge that can guide you to the start of your million dollar journey.

My journey, and all the lessons learned from it, began when I was halfway through seventh grade.

→ Snow day!

I moved from California to Northern Virginia in the middle of seventh grade. I experienced so many new concepts, including getting a foot of snow two to three times a year, which closed down schools.

One of the first times that I earned my own money was when school was out for a snow day. Unprepared for snow and still swaggering about like I was a Californian, I threw on my colorful cotton bucket hat and sunglasses and went outside to shovel the sidewalk. We didn't even have a snow shovel, so I used a garden shovel my dad had in the shed.

We lived in a townhouse community so we didn't have a driveway to shovel, but my mom made me shovel the front stoop, sidewalk, and around the car. In all, it took about a half hour. While I was outside shoveling, I realized that a lot of my neighbors hadn't shoveled yet. It seemed like an opportunity.

The process to get my first customer was simple. I walked up to the door and rang the doorbell. When they opened the door, I asked if they wanted their sidewalk shoveled. The going price? Ten bucks, and almost everyone accepted. When I was done shoveling, I knocked on the door again and received my payment.

It was fairly easy work, fast, and I enjoyed it, so I repeated the process. I got several more customers that first day and shoveled snow for hours. After I'd shoveled a few neighbors' sidewalks, I'd had my fill for the day. I put the shovel back and walked around until I joined my friends to play in the snow. They got more playtime than I did, but I had about forty dollars in my pocket, and they didn't! And forty dollars is a ton of money when you're in seventh grade.

It snowed more that night, and the next day I was able to get more shoveling gigs. I even went back to some of my customers from the previous day to freshen up their sidewalks. I gave them a discount since most of the heavy lifting had already been done. Repeat business for the win!

Each time it snowed I went out shoveling. It was easy money, and there wasn't much competition. But it was also not exactly a predictable income source.

Coming by opportunities can be simple if you're willing to look for them. As a teenager, you're willing to do almost anything to make a few bucks. Why does that ambition dissolve as we age?

→ **Lawnmower man**

As the winter turned to spring, my neighbors and I had a new problem.

Each homeowner was responsible for maintaining their small front and back yards, and everybody's lawns were now growing. We had a gas push lawn mower, and my parents assigned me the chore of cutting our grass. Like shoveling the snow in the winter, cutting grass was fairly quick because of the small yards. It only took me about twenty minutes to cut and trim my front and back yards.

I recognized from the snow shoveling days that some of my neighbors would probably like their lawns cut. I started knocking on the doors of the neighbors who had hired me to shovel their snow a couple of months earlier. Turns out, most of them were interested in having me cut their grass as well.

I started off by charging just seven dollars to cut their front and back yards. That seemed like a good deal since it only took about twenty minutes for me to cut my lawn. We lived in an end unit which meant that I had quick access to go between the front and back yards.

But only about one in ten townhouses was an end unit. That meant the majority of my customers lived in interior units, and the walk between the front yard and the back yard was pretty far and time-consuming because I had to walk all the way around several connected townhomes to get to the back. Sometimes the back gate was locked, and I had to walk back to the front, knock on the door, and ask them to open the back gate, then walk back around. When I was done cutting the back, around to the front I walked again to collect payment.

I quickly realized that I was spending about half of my time in transition from the front to back yards. The time to cut each lawn had just doubled!

I decided to raise my price. I quoted the next neighbor at ten dollars. I wasn't sure what their response was going to be, so this was a big experiment. I can only imagine how bad I delivered my sales pitch the first time I raised my rates. I was pretty nervous, but to my surprise, it worked. I had just successfully given myself a 42 percent raise and had established a new going rate. I left my old lawn mowing customers at their normal rate, but new customers paid the higher rate.

Don't be afraid to raise your prices. Many customers won't even be able to perceive the difference in small increases, especially if they are new customers and don't know your previous price.

Turns out, grass grows for more than half the year, and my customers continued to need my services. I ended up cutting about seven lawns on a regular basis that first summer.

With shoveling snow, I had discovered *reoccurring* revenue. The jobs repeated, but they were still individual projects that had defined end dates. They were also unpredictable because they depended on the weather. It was either feast or famine—a ton of work or none at all.

With cutting grass, I had discovered *recurring* revenue, at least during the long growing season. It was predictable. Every summer, customers needed my services week after week. I could plan around it.

Reoccurring revenue comes from projects which have clear start and end dates. You have to continue to find project work. Recurring revenue comes from recurring services provided to the same customer, and the need is always present.

Even though I experienced recurring revenue early in my entrepreneurial journey, the lesson did not sink in. I did not recognize the magic of the moment.

When you find yourself in a scenario where you can sell once and service the same customer over and over again, you've found recurring revenue. This is important because prospecting for new customers can be tough, time-consuming, and expensive. It's not easy to convince the prospect that you have a good offering that is worth their money. Persuading them to buy is even more difficult.

Recurring revenue is the most sought-after revenue source in the business world because the revenue continues into the future without a defined end date. Once you have customers in a recurring revenue model, your goal is to keep them there as long as possible. That means you must provide professional work with exceptional customer service. Your focus for each customer shifts from selling them to servicing them, and that's where your customers want you to focus.

You don't want to continue to sell to the same customer. Instead, you want to service that customer. As a customer, you don't want to be sold to repeatedly, but you do need the work done.

I barely started to recognize the value of customer service during my grass-cutting days. If I didn't do a good job cutting, or I failed to show up when I said I was going to (you know teenagers ... not exactly the most reliable bunch), or if I left a mess behind, then the customer was not happy with me. Although I did piss off some customers, they were quite forgiving of the neighborhood teenage boy who was hustling to make a few bucks. They almost always gave me a pass.

In retrospect, I wish they would have been tougher on me so that I recognized the consequences of screwing up. That would have helped me later in life.

→ Skate or die

By my sophomore year in high school, I was big time into skateboarding. I wanted a new skateboard, and it wasn't going to be cheap. I didn't even bother asking my parents for the money because I knew they'd say no to such an expensive toy. I was no longer cutting grass, so I needed another way to raise money.

I had noticed in school that if a kid wanted candy and didn't have any at the time, they would be willing to pay another kid for their candy. I conducted an experiment. I got on my bike and rode to the local grocery store. Looking around the candy aisle, I found bags of Blow Pops. If you're not familiar with Blow Pops, they are rather large lollipops that have a gum-filled center.

I bought a bag of Blow Pops and brought them to school the next day. I wasn't sure how to price them, so I started at fifty cents each. Sure enough, kids were interested and bought them. I sold out of that first bag, so I bought more that afternoon and sold out again the following day.

Each time I sold my Blow Pops, I'd almost always sell just one Blow Pop at a time. That led to two problems for me. The first was that I wasn't selling much to each customer. I wanted each kid to buy more than one and to make more money with each sale. The second problem was that I needed a lot of coins because most people gave me a dollar, and I had to make change for them.

So I tried a new pricing model. In addition to selling them for fifty cents each, I also sold them three for a dollar. The response? Almost everyone bought three for a dollar. In one fell swoop, I had addressed several problems. I was selling more to each customer, the value proposition had increased, and I didn't have to make nearly as much change!

Figure out what's stopping your customers from buying from you. If you think it's the price, try a different price or a different way of pricing. Make it easy for someone to buy from you, and make sure they find value in your offering.

Quickly, I stopped selling Blow Pops individually and only sold three for a dollar. Business was brisk, and after about two weeks, I had made the $150 I needed for my new bad-ass skateboard! I made my money just in time too. The principal had caught on to what I was doing, which was against school rules, so I stopped before getting busted.

Of course, I'm not recommending that you try to slide under the legal radar in your business dealings, but I am hoping you're following along with the lessons I learned about finding nearby opportunities. Since you are an entrepreneur, I am sure you have similar stories about your early business endeavors as well.

Be on the lookout for problems to solve. Be resourceful and you'll likely find a way to earn money quickly. Above all else, don't get busted by the principal!

→ Measured mile

Fast forward several years. After graduating from Virginia Tech with a BS in civil engineering, I became a construction project manager. Years passed by, I got married, and we bought an old house. I had the skills to do most of the renovation work myself, but also needed to hire a few contractors. I had a hard time finding qualified contractors and came up with an idea.

At the time, around 1999, the internet was just starting to catch on. I thought ... *Wouldn't it be cool if there was a website where homeowners like me could find qualified contractors to hire?* Think Angie's List, but in the early internet days before many people, including me, had heard of it.

I didn't know how to build a website, but I knew that the local Barnes & Noble had a huge book section on programming. I bought several books, read each cover to cover, and slowly started to build a website.

I bought the name measuredmile.com for the website. A measured mile is a term previously used by engineers that referred to the exact length of a mile. In other words, it was the standard that others were measured against. I thought that was clever and went with it. I kept playing with the website, making it more complex each time I sat down. I poured hours into it most nights and weekends, and it slowly grew more sophisticated.

At one point I had a problem with the user registration page. That page contained a password field, which was masked so someone could not see what had been typed into it, and a second masked field used to confirm they typed in the same password. Problem was, I had no idea how to compare what they entered into each field to ensure they were the same.

Realizing I was stuck, I hired a freelancer to solve the problem. He gave me the code that compared the password fields and provided the user with feedback if the fields weren't the same. I studied his code up and down and had him explain to me what it was doing before I added it to the website.

As I kept running into other programming obstacles, I went back to him for more help. Again he'd code the solution and give it to me to add to the website. And as usual, I'd study it inside out. Within a few weeks, he was providing less in the way of actual code solutions and more in the way of giving me ideas on how to solve coding problems myself. He had turned into a mentor, and my programming abilities improved rapidly.

I wasn't sure how I could make money from the website, but I knew I had to try! I hadn't spent all that time and money just for fun. I had created a marketplace of buyers (the homeowners) and sellers (the contractors), but I didn't have either of them on the website yet. I had the proverbial chicken and egg problem. How could I get buyers without sellers, and vice versa?

I volunteered to create accounts for several contractors I worked with at my day job as a construction project manager. With that, half of my marketplace was seeded. I started to get traffic to the website, including homeowners, and they were even requesting projects of contractors. Slowly but surely, more homeowners and contractors signed up. Contractors were getting leads and making money, but I wasn't!

I had heard of affiliate marketing and decided to give it a shot. Affiliate marketing is where you send someone to a third-party website, and you get a small commission if they buy something.

At the time, Amazon.com had already branched out into other items beyond books. I joined their affiliate program and found that they had a bunch of construction-related books and tools, such as cordless drills and tape measures, that I could post to my site.

When someone clicked from my site to Amazon and bought something, then I'd make a small amount. By small amount, I mean it. One holiday shopping season I made a whopping twenty bucks in commissions from Amazon!

Eager to make more money from my Measured Mile idea, I even tried selling banner ads to local businesses. A mortgage company owner reached out to me and bought a banner ad for thirty dollars a month. I created the image for the ad, posted it to my homepage, and sent them a bill for the thirty dollars. After months of asking for payment for the ad, and after months of him ghosting me, I gave up trying to collect from him. In retrospect, it would have been a good idea to collect payment before publishing his ad.

The website was live for years, but it never took off. In the end it was a financial failure. I spent $5,000 on the freelancer and made less than $100 back. Even though I had created a pretty good website that could have been useful to a lot of people, I just didn't know how to get enough people interested in it.

Contrary to the movie *Field of Dreams*, I built it but they did not come.

Frankly, my marketing chops at the time needed some serious help. I knew the product was good, but what good was it if I didn't know how to let people know about it? It seemed like a solid product wasn't enough; solid marketing was required as well. Not having a solid marketing plan was a mistake I'd repeat more than once before it sank in.

- → How are you going to let people know about your creation?
- → Where will customers come from?
- → How much money will you spend in marketing?
- → Will all the effort and cost be worth it in the end?

Even though the website was a bust, I had learned a valuable skill—computer programming. Sometime later, as I got frustrated with the construction industry and saw my friends making fortunes in IT, I switched careers to programming. So the experience proved incredibly valuable after all. I put in hundreds of hours and spent thousands of dollars, but I now could command a higher salary in an emerging and exciting field.

After a couple of years as a programmer, I knew I was one of the better programmers out there. I loved coding, but I also felt like my career was drifting along in random directions. I wasn't sure where all of this was going. Although I knew I had talent, I also felt pent-up and frustrated.

At the time, I wasn't aware that I was on a journey, but I was. My work in snow shoveling, mowing lawns, and selling candy gave me general business knowledge. My early work in building websites gave me specific knowledge on how to use the internet to build a business. Both types of knowledge—general and specific—were critical for my path to success. Both types will be critical to your success as well.

Like me, you likely have experiences from your past that you can now look back on with more mature eyes and recognize the rich learning experiences for what they were. When you connect your past experiences with your present, the combined value comes into sharper focus.

→ Where are you going?

I'm a firm believer that entrepreneurs need general business knowledge, as well as a specialization in a field, before they launch their own company. It takes time and experience to understand how business works.

In your general learning phase, it's key to learn how to work with other people. You can be a technical genius with a strong skill, but if you don't have a basic understanding of human nature and communication skills, then you are bound to bump into issue after issue when trying to scale your brilliance beyond yourself.

You also need real-world experience in a specific area. If you don't already have a hard skill, or a skill you're passionate enough about to dedicate the next decade or more to, then start studying and practicing. You need to know where you are going and in what specific area you want to become an expert.

I've changed careers three times now (not counting my teenage endeavors). Starting as a civil engineer, I transitioned to software developer and then into a digital marketer. With each of those transitions, I studied the industry that I was moving into.

When I most recently transitioned to digital marketing, I first followed online influencers in the industry. I wanted to understand what they thought was important. That led to a need for a deeper understanding of industry topics, so I subscribed to multiple industry magazines and read books by famous copywriters and ad men.

Little by little, I learned more, applied my learnings, and honed my craft. Enough so that eventually I started hosting in-person marketing meetups and addressing audiences in the marketing community. I knew where I was going, even if I didn't know my exact path to get there.

Chapter takeaways

1. The difference between reoccurring revenue and recurring revenue is significant.
2. Recurring revenue aligns your interests with your customers' interests.
3. When you're on the lookout for opportunity, you'll often find it right in front of you.
4. If you can solve someone's problem, they'll pay you for the solution.
5. When you want to buy something new, try to find a way to raise the money you need.
6. When stuck, find an expert who can get you unstuck.
7. It's better to get paid upfront than to hope to get paid afterward.
8. Not everything you try in business will be a success. But each experience provides you with both general and specific business skills that you will use later in your journey.
9. Leverage your past business experience to start surveying the entrepreneurial journey that lies ahead of you.

03 PAVING THE ENTREPRENEURIAL PATH

ERIK J. OLSON

→ MILLION DOLLAR JOURNEY

→ 04

Taking your first steps on the path to $1M

Now you've heard my early experiences, successes, and missteps. Those paved my path to growing my million dollar business. Similar to my story, you, too, can apply your past experiences to take your first steps on your entrepreneurial journey.

→ Pick your business

The early stage of your entrepreneurial journey is exciting. You're full of piss and vinegar and ready to take on the world. You're ready to start a company, to stop working for the man (or woman), and to bet on yourself.

If you're like so many others, at this point you know you want to go into business for yourself. But what business will you get into? Each of us possesses a unique combination of skills. Our experiences, career choices, and passions result in a hodgepodge of skills that could form the basis of a company.

When I was ready to strike out on my own, I was skilled in construction project management, software development, and even had experience helping my wife run her bakery business. Any, or all, of those skills could have been the basis for my new business.

You may be tempted to launch a business that incorporates all of your skills and passions. But resist the temptation to form such a broad business. I promise you: it will quickly lead to problems.

In my case, that would have meant launching a business that somehow incorporated my construction, software, and bakery experiences into one. Although that might have been wonderful for me, there were many reasons why it wouldn't work.

First, it would be hard for me to explain what my business does. The harder it is to explain your business, the less inclined potential customers will be to figure it out. If it's not caveman simple to understand what your business does, people won't invest the mental energy required to make sense of it. You want people to have a very clear, unambiguous understanding of exactly what you do, and that means simplifying your offering.

Second, what would I sell? Those three unique skills, which don't make a whole lot of sense together, were acquired over random events in my life. What exactly would I sell that combined my unique skills?

Third, it'd be nearly impossible to find and hire other people who possess that unique combination of skills and interests. If I couldn't find others with that unique combination of skills, then it would be hard for me to scale beyond my own bandwidth.

It's best to pick just one skill or one passion as the basis for your company. At most, two, but one is best. Which one or two of your skills and passions will you choose? This is the tough question that only you can answer.

"Should I do this, or do that?"

"I'm good at so many things. I can't decide what to do."

I frequently hear questions and statements like these from new entrepreneurs who can't decide what type of business to start. They think about it, analyze it, and think about it some more. But then, inevitably, they get analysis paralysis. Some may linger in this state of indecision for years. Others, forever.

One of my former co-workers talked about starting a business and going back to school to get a master's degree. That was twenty years ago, and he's yet to have started either. Think too long about what you're going to do, and you'll likely talk yourself in circles and never do anything.

My advice is to pick something you have a passion for. Reflect on your formative years and your career experiences to date, and pick the area of your life that you'll focus on for the foreseeable future.

If you're lucky and you already have an inkling of what you want to do, go forward with your idea. Be brave! It may not be the best choice (time will tell), but it's a decision, and an exciting one. Now you can start on your journey. You'll no longer be stuck staring at the starting line. You've just removed a major barrier and taken a giant step forward on your journey.

It's better to get started, even if that means potentially pivoting later, than not to get started at all. I know you don't want to be like my old co-worker who pondered it for twenty years instead of taking action! Once you're moving forward with your business, then you'll get feedback from prospects and customers, and you'll have more information to act on. That feedback will inform future decisions and will likely lead you to tweaking the plan for your journey.

After you've selected which of your passions to pursue for your new business, and after you've learned enough about the industry you've selected, next it's time to jump into the game. But how do you get experience before going all-in?

A great way to start gaining momentum is through freelancing.

→ Freelancing

Freelancing, also referred to as moonlighting, a side gig, or getting your hustle on, is when you work on a project for someone who is not your full-time employer. This kind of work is typically done on nights and weekends or whenever you're not working your full-time job.

Freelancing is a great way to make extra money while exploring if you really want to pursue the passion you chose for your entrepreneurial journey. Freelancing was my first actionable step on the path I took to my million dollar journey.

If you'll be providing a service, then freelancing is a great option for you to gain the experience you'll need and to make extra money. If you'll be providing a product instead, then freelancing really means selling your product "on the side" to friends and family, at a farmers' market, or through an established retailer.

After working as a software developer for fifteen-plus years, I began looking for freelancing opportunities online. I quickly found a website that connected freelancers to people wanting to hire a freelancer. It was called Elance—the website later merged with oDesk and rebranded to Upwork.

I created a freelancer profile and submitted bids on three or four gigs. The next day, I applied for another three or four gigs. To my amazement, I won two of these projects. Within days, I had two of my own clients. Once I decided to take action, action happened quickly.

It turned out to be more work than I was ready to take on in addition to my day job. But I didn't care. I wanted as much freelance work as possible because I had a feeling it was going to be the way out of my day job. Those first two gigs were just what I needed to get the ball rolling.

Having a day job meant that I could only work on my freelancing on nights and weekends. It's a typical entrepreneurial pattern—you have a day job that pays the bills, and you have a side gig that provides extra income and experience.

But what if you don't want to work nights and weekends? Well, it's certainly an option to quit your job before you've accumulated cash, experience, and clients, but it's an option with a ton of risk. An unnecessary risk, in my opinion. But sometimes, and to some people, it's worth it. That's your call.

For me, I prefer to take calculated risks and to lower risk when I can.

That's why freelancing was a great way forward. Freelancing nights and weekends for a few months was a minor sacrifice in order to launch my business while reducing the future risk from quitting my day job.

The extra income from freelancing was nice, but that's not why I took on those first two projects. They weren't even great projects. They were pretty terrible, actually, built with old technologies that most freelancers didn't want to work on. Yet I was eager to work with those old technologies because I wanted the experience of freelancing, and I wanted to start building my clientele. I was willing to work on lame projects to start the process of building my own company.

What most freelancers saw as a negative, I saw as a positive because I had a desire to build my experience from the ground up. These two projects would be gateway projects that I would parlay into more work with these and other clients. I was building my base, and I knew that if I did a good job on these first two projects, these clients would give me glowing testimonials that I could use as validation for wooing the next set of clients. I'd also have a portfolio of projects that I could claim as my own.

Just like in my days of shoveling snow and cutting grass, both of these clients had additional work for me after the first projects. Never one to turn down an opportunity, I took on as much as they gave me. More nights and weekends passed, and I continued to please them with my work. As expected, when I sought another client and needed a testimonial, both clients were happy to assist. The plan was working.

While I continued to bust my butt on nights and weekends, I was still working my day job as a Navy contractor. I knew the rebid on the Navy contract was approaching soon, and the end of my cushy day job and predictable income could be near. I stashed away all the cash from the side gigs into a newly formed business bank account. I didn't need the money at the time, but I knew that one day soon I would. If the rebid didn't go my way, then I had a viable option to continue freelancing. If the rebid did go my way, then I had options.

After working on that contract for nine long years and doing mostly the same thing day in and day out, I knew it was time for a change. But the money ... it was so good! Why was I even thinking of leaving such a well-paying job? What force was driving me to something else?

More importantly, how could I live with myself if I opted for the safety of my cushy job but was miserable for the rest of my career? I knew it was time to leave, but man was it hard to pull the trigger.

If you find yourself in a similar place, where you know it's time to leave your job behind so that you can pursue your own business, then it's imperative to plan your exit.

Too many times, I've seen people make rash decisions to quit their job and open their business in a rush and without a plan. But then they struggle to find work, the launch fizzles, and they run out of money. Going from being a full-time employee to running your own business is less about the event of quitting your job and starting a company, and much more about transitioning from one phase of your life to another.

Transitioning over time is the key. Rush this transition and you will suffer financially and emotionally. Do not quit your day job before you have enough clients lined up, you've saved up for the transition, and you're prepared for a dip in your income. How much you save is up to you. It all comes down to how much risk you are willing to take. For a period of time, you likely won't be making quite as much money running your own business as you were making as a full-time employee.

Your goal in planning your exit is to plan for a manageable dip in income and mitigate the risks as much as possible. Plan your transition, work nights and weekends for a while, save money, and build up your clientele. Then when you cut loose from your day job, you'll have a runway of income from existing clients, a few bucks saved, and an established portfolio and testimonials.

Don't be in a rush. Plan ahead. Move methodically, but always keep moving.

In other words, be patient, but get on with it.

→ Are you faking it?

If you're not 100 percent sure of what you're doing … if you're still trying to figure it out … welcome to the club. The reality is that most business owners who you look up to are still winging it to a certain degree.

Sure, they may have figured out the basics by now, but they didn't know squat in the beginning. Ask them, and they'll tell you about all the mistakes they made. Shoot, I'm writing *Million Dollar Journey* about all the mistakes I made! Trust me when I say that none of us knew what we were doing in the beginning.

What you're feeling right now has a name. It's called Imposter

Syndrome. You feel like you're in over your head. Like you're faking it. Like you don't know what you're doing. Chances are, at this early stage, you're partly right. But so what! What other option is better than moving forward?

Yes, it's a bit scary. But you will figure this out over time. And besides, what's the worst-case scenario? If you fail, you can always get another job. It's not that big of a deal. When you look at it like that, it's not so risky, is it? Realizing that your worst-case scenario is that you'll simply get another day job should provide you with a major confidence boost.

Here's a tip: You've heard the term "fake it 'til you make it," right? Don't do that. When you fake it, you know it and others know it too. If you lack some experience or some confidence, just own it. Tell others the truth about where you are on your journey. They'll respect you more for that and will often even help you get to the next level.

→ When to go all-in

The decision to quit your day job and go all-in on your new business is a tough one for anyone to make. Regardless of how long you've worked at your current job, or worked in general, you've become accustomed to the lifestyle that your steady paycheck has provided.

People regularly ask me about when it's the right time to go all-in on a business. First, be sure that you want your new business more than you just want to walk away from your old job. If your strongest desire is to leave your existing job more than to start your own business, then maybe what you want is a new job working for someone else. If so, that's 100 percent okay. Search for a new job instead.

But if you've concluded that, yes, what you really want is to start a business, then the next step is to evaluate your finances. Everyone has different financial needs.

If you're single and just out of school, then you can probably live on a modest income and savings. Much more so than someone with a spouse, children, a mortgage, and a car payment. Everyone has a different risk tolerance. How much or how little money you've saved up is a big factor in how much risk you will feel comfortable taking.

A young, single entrepreneur may be happy with a $1,000 buffer in the bank account. Someone in his fifties may get uncomfortable if his bank account falls below $20,000. What makes you comfortable or uncomfortable comes from your own personal perspective.

As for me, I freelanced on and off for years. My general rule was to take the payments from freelancing and put them into a business checking account. I'd only use funds from that account to pay for legitimate business expenses, but never for living expenses. By the time I decided to go all-in and quit my day job, I had saved $50,000. That may sound like a lot, but I was preparing for the worst—potentially no income coming in for long periods of time—and I needed that money to support my family and so I could stay in business.

I'm sure you've heard stories of founders selling everything they had, or draining their savings accounts and 401(k)s to start their companies. Those tales are impressive ... when they succeed. Others can have their glory. I needed security and that meant stockpiling a cash reserve from freelancing.

Your situation is your own, and you'll likely have certain lines you don't want to cross. Saving a buffer is a great way of jumping in with both feet while also wearing a life preserver. A buffer is a great way for you to focus on building your new business while not having the stress of possible total financial failure.

With a burning desire to work for myself, $50K in the bank as a buffer, and knowing I had more demand for my services than I could currently supply, that's when I decided to pull the trigger. And the timing could not have been better. When the Navy contract rebid was announced, I was on the losing side of it.

What was once a hard decision for me to make—to quit my well-paying day job or not—rather abruptly wasn't a decision at all. I was getting the boot. The winning contractor was cleaning house and bringing in their own people. In essence, I was fired. Dismissed. No longer needed. I was on my own. Having foreseen this possibility six months in advance, I was fully prepared. It was the perfect opportunity to launch my own business, and everything had lined up according to plan.

By then I had a few clients, money in savings, and an established business website, and I was bringing in about 50 percent of the income I used to get from my day job. That was enough for me to feel comfortable jumping in with both feet.

Had I not prepared in advance, had I not anticipated this event happening, I would not have been able to transition into freelancing full time so quickly.

→ Your reputation precedes you

There's truth in that saying. An excellent reputation will help you successfully launch your new business.

I had established a reputation as a hard worker through my employment at various companies and my side gigs along the way. That reputation carried over into my new business, and as word got out that I was freelancing, opportunities started to come my way.

Reputation is a funny thing. This was never more evident than a few months after I started working for myself. I got a referral for a rather nice-sized project soon after beginning freelancing full time. While I was busy working with my first few clients, a local company was looking around for someone to help them on a new project. Someone I knew found out about the project and recommended me to the client because of my reputation. Not only did my reputation precede me, it brought me leads!

Whenever possible, make decisions that will positively affect your reputation. When you need to make a tough decision or hold a difficult conversation, do so in a way that won't damage your reputation. Once damaged, it's nearly impossible to recover your reputation.

→ Multiple personas

Did you know that you have multiple professional personas? Most entrepreneurs do, especially in the beginning.

During my early entrepreneurial journey, I accumulated various contexts, aka personas, for how people knew me. I was Erik the Navy contractor, but I was also freelancing on side projects. Most people knew me by one of those personas, but others knew me from my involvement in professional organizations, or because they were customers from previous side gigs, or from one of the products I had launched.
By this point, my personas were ...

- → An employee on a Navy project.
- → A freelancer who takes on side gigs.
- → Someone who took on side gigs under a company name I had formed years earlier.
- → A board member of a nonprofit

professional organization.
→ A person who built a web application for other members of his nonprofit to use for free.
→ A bakery co-owner with my wife, working there some nights and most weekends.
→ Owner of multiple online businesses, including Measured Mile.

Each business relationship I had with someone was under a different context. Within each context, I operated under a persona.

My guess is that you're in a similar situation. Living with multiple personas means that you haven't projected a consistent message of who you are to the world. The world perceives you differently based on which persona you project at any given time. Having multiple personas means there's an opportunity to do a much better job at branding who you are.

The most distinct personas are that of a full-time employee and freelancer. Those are two worlds you don't want to collide. You don't want your employer to find out that you are freelancing, and you don't want your freelance clients to know much, if anything, about your day job. You have to keep those two personas separate.

As a consequence, people are often reluctant to talk openly about what they do. For example, you probably only post about your day job persona on LinkedIn. If you choose to post about being an employee, then your freelance prospects will be confused and may not hire you. But if you post about being a freelancer on your LinkedIn profile, and your company finds out, your job may be in jeopardy.

What do most people do with their multiple personas? They keep those personas as far away from each other as they can. In the end, they do a terrible job of marketing themselves because they can't safely project the right persona in a public setting.

A friend of mine runs a limo company. That's his side gig, and he also has a full-time corporate job. In order to ensure that his two worlds do not collide, he won't associate his name or face with his limo business. He just can't risk people at work finding out about the limo company. The result is that he cannot openly talk about his limo business in public or online, and he can't parlay his own personal reputation, his own personal brand, to get him business. He knows it's holding back the growth of his limo business, but he doesn't want to risk people at work knowing what he's up to on the side.

The longer you don't tell your network about your side gig, freelancing, or new company, the longer you're working at a disadvantage. At this early stage in your business, your network is gold, and you need to activate it to get new customers.

The sooner you can transition to working your side hustle full time, the sooner you can do away with your day job persona. That persona, which has served you well in the past, is now holding you back the most.

The day I walked away from my day job was the day I finally ditched my employee persona. Once I ditched that persona, I knew I had to consolidate all my other personas. I needed everyone I knew to start thinking about me as the guy running his own business. Not as the full-time employee. Not as the baker's husband. Not as the nonprofit member. I needed everyone to know me for the business I was launching, and that's it.

In order to consolidate down to that one main persona, I started by shutting down old email accounts and old websites. These were mostly from when I had previously attempted to launch companies. I had those email addresses rerouted to my new business's email address and old websites rerouted to my new company website. With that, I ended the lingering personas of "Erik, the part-time freelancer." I shut down several personas where I was a small-time, part-time freelancer and replaced them all with the persona of being a full-time business owner.

Some side projects, like Measured Mile, were still lingering around at the time. Even though those side projects occasionally brought in a small amount of revenue, it was time to let them go. I no longer wanted to be associated with those side projects and didn't want to put any more time into them. So I shuttered them all. I shut down Measured Mile and other similar side projects. That got rid of another old persona—the guy who ran a bunch of small-time websites.

Then I looked at each of my social media profiles. I updated where I worked on sites like LinkedIn, Facebook, and Twitter. I shared my new company, and I updated LinkedIn to show that I no longer worked at my old day job. Once I cleaned up my personas and consolidated down to one, I was ready to come out of the closet with my new business.

This is where you, too, can begin to trim down those extra personas: in your websites, email addresses, and social media accounts. When you're ready to go all-in, then it's time to present your new consolidated persona to the world.

Chapter takeaways

1. Don't start a business that encompasses all of your skills and passions. Pick one—two at most—as the core of your business offering.
2. Find online gigs and freelance work before quitting your day job. That'll earn you money and get you real-world experience you can build on.
3. Don't rush to quit your day job. Plan your transition, save money, and prepare for a temporary reduction of income as your new business gets going.
4. Don't fake it 'til you make it. Be transparent, and others will help you along your journey.
5. Shut down old personas once you go all-in and quit your day job. Your network needs to know you as the business owner who's starting a new business.

→ MILLION DOLLAR JOURNEY

Branding

Your brand, whether personal or business, is a reflection of you unto the world. And I'm not just talking about your company name or logo. Your brand encompasses everything you project out to others, and it's how people perceive and interact with you.

A good brand is created intentionally, not haphazardly. Think through pros and cons of decisions, such as company names, your website, the services you'll provide, and your overall tone and demeanor. What do you stand for? What problems do you solve? What values do you project?

But like anything else in business, don't allow analysis to paralyze you. Think about it, decide quickly, and implement. As time goes on, you'll refine your brand and maybe even pivot entirely.

→ The importance of your company name

You've probably obsessed over what to name your business. I have spun up several different businesses in the past. Each time I came up with a business idea, I immediately focused on what to name the business.

This is common with entrepreneurs. Everybody wants a cool and unique name, and everybody thinks that the name is super important to your success. But here's a dirty little secret. It doesn't matter all that much.

Think about some of the brands you follow, buy from, or are familiar with. Here are a few large brands to consider: Google, GE, Verizon, Apple, Walmart, IKEA, Angie's List, Craigslist, eBay, and Amazon. These are iconic brands, and you may think these are amazing company names. But are they really?

Let's take Apple, for instance. Is that a great name? If I told you I was opening a business and I was going to name it Grape, would you think I'm a genius or would you think I'm crazy? My guess is you would think I'm crazy. Why would I name my business after a fruit?

So then why do you think Apple is an amazing name for a company that makes computers and other electronic products? The company may be great, and they may have a great brand, but the reality is that it's not an amazing name for a business. The brand is amazing, but the company name is simply a reference to the brand. If the same company had originally been named Grape, and you always knew it as Grape, then you'd likely think it to be just as good of a name as you currently consider Apple to be.

Let's look at another example: Walmart. Is that a great name? Hardly. Walmart is a concatenation of Walton, the founder's last name, and "mart" which is short for market. What if I were to tell you that I was going to open a supermarket and call it Olsmart. Would you think it's a great name? I seriously doubt it.

The Walmart name has morphed numerous times over the years. Sam Walton's first store was named Walton's Five and Dime. A descriptive name at best, they named their second location Wal-Mart. More recently it's been tweaked to Walmart. Although a great and iconic brand, its name is simplistic and rudimentary. But even a brand as large as Walmart has needed to pivot its company name over time.

Another example of a terrible name that's stuck is eBay, one of the earliest internet auction websites. Think that eBay is a great name? Why?

eBay is short for Echo Bay. "Bay" refers to the San Francisco Bay area where founder Pierre Omidyar lived. When he created the online auction website, he wanted the domain name echobay.com, but it was taken, so he went with the shorter name eBay.com. Although eBay is a well-known name now, I would argue that it's a terrible name to give your business.

Let's say I copied eBay's logic when naming a company and its website. The region that I live in calls itself The 757 after the area code assigned to most phones locally. If I were to call my company The 757 and got the website address—aka domain name—t757.com, would that be good? Locally, it has a small chance of working, but only because people here get it. People outside of this region have no idea what The 757, or t757 is. I imagine you would agree that would be a bad company name, but the logic worked out for eBay.

One last example: Amazon. It's a fantastic brand, and many people think it's a fantastic name in general. But let's think about it. The company is named after a river in South America. Can you envision what the Amazon River looks like? Can you envision exactly where it is on the globe or in what direction it runs? Most people are so unfamiliar with the Amazon River that they don't know the basics about it. But they do know that it's the longest river in the world. Or is it? The Amazon River, in fact, is the second longest river in the world after the Nile River.

What if I were to open a business and name it after something vaguely understood by the population … something notable for being the second longest or tallest in the world? What if instead of the world's longest rivers I went with the world's tallest trees?

Many probably know that the sequoia is the tallest tree in the world. Sequoia could make a great company name. But no—we're going to name it after the second tallest tree—the yellow meranti. Would that name be associated with a tall tree and give the company the prominence it desires? I don't think so, but that logic seemed to work out for Amazon.

See, these names just don't matter all that much. Certainly, you don't want a terrible name, but as long as it's an okay name, it will work out if you build a great brand around it. No matter what, some people will think your new company name is great, and others will think it's stupid. But the better the brand you create, the fewer people will think that the name is stupid. In the end, the name itself is simply a pointer to your reputation as a company.

All that said, you will spend time trying to find a good company name. And you should. Although I just said it doesn't matter, it matters to you, so it matters.

Let's see how you can go about picking a good company name.

→ Selecting your company name

You can choose your company name via several methods. The most simplistic type of name is one that describes what you offer.

Let's say you are opening a window cleaning business. In this case, a descriptive company name would be something like: We Clean Windows, or Clear Window Cleaning Company. It's clear (pun intended) what you do. That's the positive.

The negative of that name is that it lacks creativity. It "feels" like a commodity. Like a name that any person anywhere in the world may use. It's not unique at all. It sounds like a normal phrase you may even use in a sentence. There's little branding value to it, and from a digital marketing perspective, it would be hard to create SEO (search engine optimization) value from that common name.

That is one reason some companies sport an outlandish name and others invent names. Etsy, the online marketplace for creators, is a completely nonsensical name by design. The creator wanted a made-up name to guarantee uniqueness.

Another way you can pick a company name is to look for a synonym, or even an antonym, of the descriptive name. Again, let's say you are opening a window-cleaning business. What's a synonym for window? Maybe something like glass, window pane, storefront, or the phrase "see through." All these words are close in meaning to the word "window," they are still descriptive, yet they are also a bit creative.

Many times I have leveraged an online dictionary to find alternative names to a descriptive word I have in mind. I'll look at the definition of the word, its synonyms and antonyms, and search for variants of the name I started with. All that searching will lead to new words and new ideas. I recommend you do the same. You may not find exactly what you're looking for, but it will give you lots of ideas to pull from. What you're looking for is something that "feels" right and sounds great.

Once you have some ideas, take a look around your market to see if others use a similar or even conflicting name. This makes for good intel and is much better to have before you announce your new name rather than after. Also be sure to check online to see if someone else has a trademark for your names. Trust me, I've made that mistake before! I'll go into that story in a minute.

Everybody wants to start with the perfect company name. I get it. Try to launch with a great name, but know that it doesn't matter that much. It's not a deal-breaker one way or the other.

What's important here is to pick a name that is somewhat creative, has some unique quality to it, that doesn't conflict with other competing or local company names, and provides at least a small hint of your offering. Spend a couple of days doing light research. Come up with lots of different options.

Then just pick one. Really, that's what it'll come down to. Your gut intuition. It may not be your perfect forever name, but for now it's good enough. Once you decide, that's one less obstacle to starting your business. Just pick a name and get started.

→ Rebranding

Here's another secret: You can easily rename your company. You can do this by filing for a DBA—a Doing Business As—certificate.

A DBA is a formal way for the government to allow you to operate a business under another name. The last time I got a DBA in my city, it only cost ten dollars. Operating as a DBA is a fast, inexpensive, and easy way to either launch a new brand for your company or to completely rebrand.

I've rebranded companies two times. Learn from my mistakes to avoid making them yourself.

My first experience with rebranding a company was when I realized that the name of my first company, Fresh Information Management Systems, or FreshIMS for short, didn't hit the mark. That name was a mouthful and didn't resonate with anyone.

When I started to think about a new company name, I began by doing a lot of dictionary and synonym research. I Googled to try to find ideas and inspiration for a new name. I looked at what other companies in my industry had done and tried to figure out what would be hip. I wanted a short name, one that was not a literal description of my offering, and one that was somewhat abstract.

After considering many options, I settled on the name "80/20" as a new company name. This name was short, cool, abstract, and related to my industry (business people tend to refer to the 80/20 Rule). I filed for a DBA and announced to the world my new company name. Unfortunately, I immediately encountered problems.

As a result, I now ask the following questions when branding or rebranding a company.

1. Is there another company with the same or a similar name?

It is vital that you conduct research to find out if any other companies use the name that you're considering, or something close to it.

I didn't discover until a month after committing to 80/20 that another company, the 80/20 Burger Bar, operated in the same city. Although I wasn't aware of its existence, it was apparently a pretty popular restaurant and quite a few people were familiar with that name. This caused its fair share of problems for my business. It was sometimes confusing to people when I introduced myself as the owner of 80/20 if they had heard of the 80/20 Burger Bar.

On one occasion, I went to the Apple Genius Bar for help with my MacBook. When asked who I worked for, I said 80/20. The employee assisting me smiled and said, "I love that place!" I found it necessary to correct her ... "The consulting company, not the burger bar," to which she replied, "Oh. I've heard of you too." I had my suspicions and said, "Really? It's okay ... it happens all the time." I was right—she admitted that she had never heard of my 80/20.

I knew I had to differentiate myself from the 80/20 Burger Bar, and fast, if I wanted to have any success in generating brand awareness around my company and attracting new customers. For this reason, I started to refer to my company as 80/20 Consulting. I wanted to stick with 80/20, but I had to tweak the name due to brand confusion.

2. **Is the domain name, or a good variant, available?**

After settling on 80/20 as the company name, I began my search for a domain name. "8020.com" had already been purchased by someone else, but they weren't using it. With the .com domain name unavailable, I searched for a variant.

I eventually landed on the domain name "8020.co." The ".co" Top Level Domain (TLD) was trending at the time, and I thought that the ".co" version of the domain name being available was a sign from above. This must be the right company name for me! I ended up buying "8020.co" and setting up a website around it.

Unfortunately, it wasn't long before I discovered that about once a month someone would think that I had mistakenly left the "m" off of ".co" in my email address. Emails to erik@8020.com bounced. People also had trouble getting to what they thought was my website, 8020.com, because they added an "m" to the end.

Apparently, people weren't as familiar with ".co" domain names as I was. When I bought company T-shirts and put "8020.co" on the back, people didn't realize it was a domain name. In later versions of the T-shirt, I felt compelled to prefix it with "www" to form "www.8020.co" so that people would realize it was a website address.

While a ".co" TLD offers more options to those in search of a domain for their business, the public just wasn't ready for it. Since it's so close to ".com," it's confusing. I eventually admitted defeat and got a new domain name, madeby8020.com. Longer, but easier to comprehend.

A few years later, I merged my company with another company. With this second rebranding, I had an opportunity to correct the branding mistakes I had made with 80/20.

3. How can you get the team involved?

Early on, my other founder and I started the brainstorming process for company names. Every few days we'd announce a new possible name to the team to gain their perspective and receive feedback.

To our surprise, no one liked the names we were picking. Although I initially thought this was likely due to the "Not Invented Here" syndrome, they pointed out bona fide issues with the names that resulted in us returning to the drawing board. Once I had the brilliant idea of naming our company The Yield Agency, where yield meant the size of a harvest. My team pointed out that yield also means to slow down and give way to others. Were we pushovers? No, that name wasn't going to work!

Realizing that the two of us were making slow progress operating in a vacuum, we decided that a group brainstorming session was in order. One of our employees volunteered to moderate the group and keep us on task.

We spent a couple of hours writing words we liked, as well as word combinations, on sticky notes. The sticky notes went up on a board and then got moved or removed based on discussion. After some time, we successfully narrowed a list of over one hundred potential names down to a short list of about ten names. Through more discussion, we kept coming back to one sticky note. That sticky note contained the lone word "Array." Once we realized that we kept coming back to that name, we also realized that it was the winner.

We had our new name ... for the time being.

4. Is anyone else using your selected name?

We liked Array and decided to go with it. The next day, I researched some more and discovered that the company name was already registered in our state to a small company in an unrelated industry a few hours away. This caused us to begin the process of looking for a close variant.

At the same time, both Kevin and I began telling our friends and family the new name we had chosen. When we told them that we had selected the name "Array," to our surprise, our friends and family didn't quite understand the word that had just come out of our mouths. We had to say it again, slower. They expected us to say more after that single word. It was like a hanging chad. It just wasn't complete by itself.

So we'd amplify by saying, "Array. You know, like array digital." Digital was one of the words on the sticky notes, but it wasn't good enough by itself. But digital after array sounded great and gave a pretty strong hint as to the kind of work the company did.

Based on the facts that "Array" was already taken, and our friends and family were a bit confused by that singular word, we decided that Array Digital was a better name. Best of all, that company name was not registered in Virginia!

With that, our new company name was locked down.

5. Who else uses that name?

An IT company in California had previously spun off a quasi-brand named Array Digital for the websites they built for their IT customers. By the time we picked Array Digital for our name, that company had already abandoned operations years earlier. That seemed like a good thing to us. After all, it's rare to find a company name that no one has ever used. We assumed that because they were no longer in operation, there shouldn't be much confusion. How wrong we were.

As it turned out, the company in California owned, and still owns, the domain names "arraydigital.com" and "arraydigital.co." Considering the fact that "arraydigital.com" was our first choice for a domain name, this was a disappointment.

I decided to reach out to them before we rebranded and offered to buy "arraydigital.com." They declined but offered to sell us the ".co" version instead. Due to my previous experience with "8020.co," I knew that a ".co" was not for me, so I passed.

We compared the pros and cons of several alternative domain names and went with "thisisarray.com." But we still preferred "arraydigital.com." Oh well. We settled into the new brand and the domain name "thisisarray.com" and went about our business.

In the end, pick a domain name, a ".com" preferably, and stick with it even if it's not a 100 percent perfect match with your company name.

→ Buying a domain name

So how do you go about buying your own domain name?

You buy domain names online from companies named registrars. There are literally hundreds of registrars you can choose to buy a domain from.

Most registrars charge between ten and thirty dollars per year for a domain name. GoDaddy is a popular domain registrar, but I prefer buying from Google Domains. They're cheap, and they include privacy protection at no cost. That means your personal information won't be publicly associated with the domain name, and your email address won't be exposed for spammers to find. You can buy from Google Domains at https://domains.google.

Once you're on a registrar's website, you'll need to search for a domain name. Ideally your domain name will exactly match your company name. But more likely than not, the domain name that you want won't be available.

Be prepared to look for an alternative domain name, just like I did for 80/20 and Array Digital, that includes some or most of your company name. Alternatively, you may even want to modify your company name to match an available domain name that you like.

Because domain names, especially those ending in ".com," are becoming rarer, some people buy domain names even before they name their companies. I'm not a fan of this technique because I believe your company name is much more important to your branding than your domain name. It's best to think about the company name and the domain name at the same time.

Make sure that your domain name is easy to say and easy for people to understand. You will have to say this domain name a lot, especially with your email address, so you want people to be able to understand it when you say it. When my wife and I launched a website for her bakery, we went with lachoclatier.com (playing off of the word chocolatier). No one knew how to spell it, and we constantly had to spell it out one letter at a time.

Keep it short. If you have to remove a few characters without losing significant value by doing so, then that's fine. With Array Digital, we could have gone with thisisarraydigital.com. Adding the "digital" would have conformed perfectly with our company name, but that would have added an extra seven unnecessary characters. Shorter is better.

Avoid dashes and numbers in your domain name. Although they are allowed, they are uncommon. If you have a dash, or an underscore, or numbers, it will confuse people. I already mentioned the name of my previous company was 80/20, but slashes aren't allowed in domain names, so a perfect match between a domain name and my company name was out of the question. Even though numbers are allowed, people are never sure if they are spelled out or not. Avoid numbers, especially at the start of a domain name, because people will think you're giving them your phone number instead of your domain name!

The goal here is to get a domain name that is a close match to your company name, is easy to say, and will not confuse people. You are going to have to live with this domain name for a while, so think through a bunch of options before you pull the trigger on one.

Chapter takeaways

1. Although finding the perfect company name seems important, it's really not all that important.
2. When picking a company name, avoid simplistic and descriptive names.
3. Search for a creative name by researching definitions, synonyms, and antonyms of words you think may work.
4. Once you land on a name that may work, check to see if a competitor has a similar name.
5. Confirm that a domain name is available that will work with your company name.
6. When brainstorming a company name, involve more people.
7. If possible, select a domain name that ends in ".com" that is a close match to your company name.

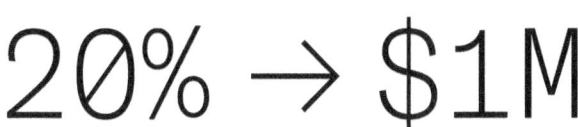

→ 06

Open for business

By now you've identified a skill that you want to focus on, you've validated your offering by getting someone to buy from you, you have a company name, you've bought a domain name, and you've started to set up your business's brand.

Time to hang your shingle and let the world know you're open for business!

Up until this point, there is little need to worry about any legalities to freelancing. But once you're ready to go out on your own, you need to think about the legal implications and jump through the necessary hoops.

→ Selecting your business entity

The phrase "business entity" refers to the legal structure of a business. As the person opening the business, you can declare that you are one of many different types of businesses. Each entity type has its pros and cons.

I am not going to go into this very deeply because you can find a ton of literature on the internet about the different kinds of business entity types.

Here are the most common types for most businesses:

- → Sole proprietor
- → S Corp
- → C Corp

Consult with the internet and an attorney to find the best entity type for the business you plan to open. But in my experience, an LLC is the best option for most companies, so we're going to dive right into that.

→ Limited liability company (LLC)

A common way of isolating business risk is to establish a limited liability company, also known as an LLC. My lawyer once told me that an LLC is like a legal firewall between you and your personal assets, and the assets and risk of your business.

Generally speaking, lawsuits and financial liabilities cannot cross that legal firewall. If someone sues your LLC for a hundred times what the LLC is worth, then they can take everything in the LLC. They can wipe it clean, but they can only take what the LLC owns. They can't cross the legal firewall, meaning they can't take your house, your retirement, or other personal assets.

There are also tax benefits to opening an LLC. Any profit (or loss) that the LLC realizes for a given tax year will not result in taxes paid by the LLC directly. Instead, those will be filed with your personal taxes, and you will file one tax return. This is a good tax scenario because you will only be taxed once for that income regardless of whether it came from regular W-2 employment, or from your LLC, or from both.

An LLC is a good business entity type for an individual business owner or a partnership. If you have a partner, then you will each own a percentage of the LLC. LLCs can even be owned by other companies.

In most states, you can get your own LLC from the state government pretty quickly online. In my home state of Virginia, I've completed the process in under ten minutes on multiple occasions. The process requires you to provide basic information about yourself and your business, such as the name and address, and to pay a small fee.

As part of becoming an LLC, you are expected to include "LLC" at the end of your company name. As an example, although I refer to my company as Array Digital, technically it's Array Digital, LLC.

For that reason, I recommend that you first get your LLC, which modifies your formal company name. Everything else you do will use the new formal name with LLC at the end.

→ Business license

A business license is a tax that you pay to the city that you reside in, or to the city in which you will conduct your business.

I find it ridiculous that you have to pay your city a tax in order to open a business. You may feel the same way. But frankly, it doesn't matter how we feel. That's life, and if you want to conduct a business legally, then you need a business license, and that means paying the tax. Local laws vary so check with your city for details.

If a business license is required in your city, but you decide not to pay the tax or not to get a business license, you are opening yourself up to a liability. If discovered, then the city will crack down hard on you. You'll end up paying the business license tax and penalties too, and they will likely compel you to stop operating your business until you're in good standing. It's not something to mess around with. Just call your city or go to their website and get your legal affairs in order.

Most cities will charge a minimum amount if you don't exceed a revenue threshold. You will typically pay something like fifty dollars for the first $100,000 in revenue. If you make more than $100,000, then your taxes will be calculated as a percentage of your gross revenue. This varies from city to city, so again, check with them for the details.

Once you have your business license, you are 100 percent free to start conducting business. Let's get to it!

→ **Tell the world**

Your network is your most powerful weapon at this early stage of starting your business. You need to activate your network and tell them what you're doing. But many instinctively hold back for a few reasons.

Although I had launched a website and updated my online profiles, most people in my network simply did not realize what I was up to until I told them. They'd literally have to stumble across my profile or website and figure it out for themselves. That wasn't good enough. You have to proactively tell your network what you're up to. Ensure they get the message so that they can begin to refer business to you.

When I launched my company, I decided that, in addition to my website and updating my online profile, I would send a letter to every person I knew who I also had a mailing address for. The idea was to send out an announcement. Almost like a wedding announcement in that it was a formal announcement.

When I say everyone I knew, I mean everyone. Anyone that I had ever come into contact with. Friends, schoolmates, past roommates, even my close friends and family who already knew what I was up to. Every single person that I could reach—I needed them to clearly understand what I was up to. Once they knew, they could potentially refer me business.

I wrote a letter and prepared to send 236 envelopes—one to each person I had an address for. I did it on the cheap and had the announcements printed at a local office shop. They also printed address labels that I would put on each envelope. Not exactly the classiest production, but the point was to get the letter, and the message, out to my world.

I felt a lot of anxiety about dropping those letters in the mailbox. Once dropped in the mail, I wouldn't be able to take them back. By announcing what I was doing to everyone I knew, I would be fully committing to my new company. And once committed to the company, I was also committed to the outcome.

What if the company failed?

By sending those announcements, I was making myself vulnerable to the shame I'd feel if the company failed. For that reason, many entrepreneurs resist telling everyone they know what they're doing. It's a way of hedging their bets in case they fail.

I can understand that, but what was much more important than potential embarrassment was seizing the opportunity to get the word out about what I was doing. I had to let the world know and also let them know that I needed their help.

The letter basically said: I've opened a business, here's what we do, and if you know anyone who needs this service then please send them my way. I didn't directly solicit my network for work, but I did ask them to refer me to people who may need my help.

Within days, everyone I knew was aware of the transition I had made. And guess what? I got a couple of new leads from the letters, and one of those leads turned into a paying gig. I had made myself vulnerable, let my entire network know that I was open for business, and as a result, I had landed another client!

The announcement was effective and cheap, costing only about $200 total for the printing and stamps. Whether you want to take the same route with mailings is up to you. But no matter what, tell the world about your new business and ask for referrals.

→ Activate your network

Many years ago, when I was still an employee, I would occasionally notice that a co-worker who was previously inactive on LinkedIn would suddenly start to get many new connections. I realized they were likely looking for a new job, which they'd confirm if I asked them in confidence. Although it's great they were reaching out to new people to connect with, they were doing it too late in the game.

Don't wait until you need your network to create your network. A network is only valuable when it's activated. Networks take time to cultivate in the first place, and you have to be connected with people and give them value first before you can ask for something in return.

Not surprisingly, my co-workers who had waited until the last minute when things were not going so well didn't have a lot of opportunities coming to them.

It made me realize that I needed to start building my network well before I went off on my own. So I started to reach out to more people online and in person. I joined professional organizations and attended meetings. My goal was to meet as many business people as I could and to cultivate that network before I needed it.

By the time I needed a network that I could reach out to for referrals, the network was there. And when I needed people to know what I was up to, I activated my network and told them.

I have continued to cultivate my network over time, and it has served me well. As an example, when I first started to think about writing *Million Dollar Journey*, I realized that I once again had to expand my network. But this time I wasn't looking for people to refer me to clients. I was looking for people who would be interested in buying a book about entrepreneurship and could tell me what they needed the most help with.

Twitter has been my go-to network for entrepreneurs. Many entrepreneurs hang out there and share their experiences and give advice on running businesses. It is the perfect network to reach people who could provide me feedback on the best entrepreneurial topics to dive into.

Starting about a year before I sat down to write the first words of *Million Dollar Journey*, I began to actively build my Twitter network even more. I reached out to many Twitter profiles, followed them, and interacted with them online, and they reciprocated by following me and interacting with my tweets. I asked a lot of questions about their biggest struggles in business and used that insight to inform my decisions about what to include and exclude from this book.

I also let my network on Twitter and beyond know that I was writing a book. Each time I sat down to write, I told them. Each time I edited a chapter, I told them. My network was on this book-writing journey with me, and they saw all of the ups and downs and how much work it is to write and publish a book. As I shared, I built anticipation for the final product.

As you prepare for your next move, think about how your network could help you. If you don't have a strong network already, start building it before you need it. Cultivate it by giving them value at every opportunity.

Give to your network first. Then when you ask something from them, they'll be more likely to help you back. You'll be surprised that people you may not even know will go out of their way to help you because you have helped them, either directly or indirectly, in the past.

→ Launch your website

A website is a critical tool for every company. Even if you don't get much traffic to it, the traffic that will go there is critical for your growth.

Each time you communicate with someone new about doing work for them, they will instinctively require validation that you are a legitimate business. This is especially true when you are a one-man or one-woman show. Although you may have a good reputation, they need to see specific validation before they will hire you.

One of the best forms of validation is your own website. Not having a website implies that you are not a legitimate company or that you are such a young company you haven't even had time to get around to launching your website. If you do not have a website, you greatly reduce your chances of winning new work.

Just having a website, even if it's horrible, is ten times better than not having a website at all. I can't stress this enough—you must have a website or people will perceive that your business is not legitimate.

Once you know your company name and what you offer, you need to act quickly to set up at least a basic website, or you'll struggle greatly to get work.

We covered your website's domain name in the last chapter. Now let's talk about the website itself.

→ DIY website builder

A quick and inexpensive way of building a website is to use a do-it-yourself (DIY) website builder. You can literally find hundreds of DIY website builders on the internet that will not cost you a lot of money. Examples include WIX, Squarespace, Weebly, GoDaddy, and many more. It does not matter which one you choose since they all provide the same basic features. Do a little bit of research, find out how much they are charging for a minimal website, and then pull the trigger and start building it yourself.

You do not need to spend a lot of time or money on the first iteration of your website. Remember, going from no website to a website is a massive improvement in your marketing and positioning. Even a basic website will pay great dividends. Create a website with three to five web pages. Don't go nuts adding a lot of pages at this point because, frankly, you won't have a whole lot to say.

You'll need at least a homepage, an About Us page, and a Contact Us page.

The homepage provides an overall summary of who you are, what you do, and why someone should hire you. Although it's a summary, it should have enough information so that people get a good sense of what your company does. People love seeing pictures of others, so I recommend including pictures of you and, if they'll agree to it, your clients.

The About Us page will go into more detail about you, your company, the types of clients you service, and other details people want to know about you. Keep it professional and centered around your work, your results, and client testimonials.

Your Contact Us page needs to provide your address, phone number, and a form that will allow people to reach out to you if they have a question but don't feel like calling at the moment. The form should collect the person's name, phone number, and email address. That is all the information that you need in order to reach back out to them. You can also include a "How can we help you?" text box if you'd like, but in my experience, that is often used by spammers to send you spam email.

Throughout your website, make sure that you add pictures of yourself, your office, your clients, and anything that's pertinent. People want to visualize who you are, where you do your work, and what your brand is all about.

Testimonials from previous projects and clients are key. When you are new, you need to provide as much validation as possible. If you have testimonials, then personalize the quotes by including the person's picture, their name, and their company name. Make it as concrete as possible.

→ Business cards

Like a website, you need business cards. Most business people have business cards on them at all times. When you come into contact with someone, you want to be able to give them a business card and receive theirs. It's a fast way to exchange contact data so you can follow up afterward.

You can find thousands of sources for business cards, both online or at a local print or office supply store. If you need business cards quickly, your local print shop can quickly design and print them for you. Although a slightly more expensive option, you'll have business cards within an hour or two.

I prefer to get business cards online. In the past we've bought from websites such as moo.com, vistaprint.com, and gotprint.com. They each have pre-existing designs to choose from, or you can design your own. They're cheap and usually arrive within a week. I typically order 250 at a time.

I found that I did not hand out a lot of business cards in the beginning. I still don't. But I want each one that I hand out to have an impact on the person who receives it. For that reason, I searched for something unique several years ago, which I ended up buying from a printer in China.

After being in business for about six months, I came across someone who had a metal business card. I was instantly intrigued and had to get one for myself. I searched the internet and found several vendors that would provide it. But the cost was significant at three-to-five-dollars each! After scouring the internet, I found them on a Chinese website, Alibaba, for a dollar each.

You may be wondering if spending a dollar on each business card was worth it. The answer is a profound, Yes.

Each time I handed out a metal business card, the conversation instantly turned toward my card. When I found myself in a large meeting where attendees passed out cards, the meeting would stop as people commented about my card. My card was different, and no one had a card like mine. Others would admit that their cards were lame compared to mine.

The great part about this is that people remembered me, and they held onto the card. Where most business cards look the same and quickly end up in someone's trash can, mine often would remain on someone's desk for months or years. They'd even show it off to others! Being a bit different with a metal business card led to a completely different experience than if I had saved a few bucks and opted for standard business cards.

Speaking of business cards, sometimes people you meet won't have a card on them. In those situations, it's common for you to give them your card and ask them to contact you.

Pro tip: Instead of hoping they follow up with you, which they're unlikely to do, ask them for their email address or phone number. Enter their contact information into your phone right then. Send them a message on the spot and confirm they received your message.

→ Office space

When I went off to work on my own as a full-time freelancer, I found myself without an office space for the first time in a long time. I had a decision to make ... where should I hang my shingle?

At the time it didn't matter where I worked from, just that I got the work done. For the first time ever, I had the freedom to work from anywhere I wanted. I wanted to keep expenses low and to work "remote" as long as possible.

I tried working from coffee shops, but they were too noisy. It also seemed silly to go to a public place but then isolate myself and zone out on my computer. I could zone out at home without having to try to ignore everything around me. Why even leave the house?

And that's what I ended up doing. I started working from home. At the time we didn't have a home office, so I had to carve out a place to work. The only good place to work was the dining room table. It was just me, a laptop, a cell phone, and my dining room table.

Every morning I'd open up my backpack, pull out my laptop, charger, and paperwork, and I'd spread it all out on the dining room table. Cell phone at the ready, I'd start working. I'd spend long stretches of time working and staring deep into my laptop screen. But quickly I discovered a problem—my family!

Since I was home and nearby, my lovely wife would occasionally pop her head in with a "quick question." Just a small distraction, no biggie, by itself. But inevitably, there were several of these quick questions throughout the day. Each would pull me out of my zone and interrupt my flow. Not the worst of problems, but still they were distractions.

My kids were still in elementary school at that time and school ended early for them. By 2:30 p.m., they were back in the house. When they came in, they were happy to see daddy and would give me hugs and kisses. Then my wife would take them in the other room so I could continue to work. Kids being kids, they were sometimes loud. That was distracting. They would sometimes roam over and show daddy something. Another distraction.

My wife would start to make dinner at about 5:30 p.m. Pots clanking. Distraction. Oven doors opening and closing. Distraction. The kids getting hangry. Distraction.

By 6 p.m. or so, it was time to eat, and I'd put everything back in my backpack so we could eat at the dining room table, which for the last few hours had served as my desk. Although I had been working all day, I was in a regular state of distraction triage. Some distractions I could ignore, others I could avoid, while others I could not. But each required some of my attention.

Working from home only lasted a week. I love my family, but I also had to focus on work when I was working.

I found a sublease on Craigslist. A small accounting firm about fifteen minutes from home had an extra room in their office. They had two small office rooms in their upstairs that they rented out for extra revenue. One was already occupied by another solopreneur, and I ended up renting the other office.

It was relatively small, maybe ten by ten feet, but it was plenty big for me. I set up a desk, a whiteboard, and a guest chair in case anyone ever came by. It had a lockable door and a window. Although the office itself was small, I could use the kitchen and bathroom downstairs.

The room cost $400 a month. Not a ton of money, but it was an extra expense that I hadn't anticipated. Although I didn't want to spend any more than necessary, I needed a distraction-free zone when I went to work. Some people work well from home, but I needed separation between work and home, and for $400, I got it. I also knew that if I couldn't afford an extra $400 a month in expenses, then something was seriously wrong with my business.

The office space worked out great for me. It was cheap, and I could close the door and get work done without distractions. But after a few months, I was getting lonely from the isolation. I often found excuses for leaving that small office, and I sought out other humans to interact with. Lingering downstairs to talk to the receptionist. Quick trips to 7-Eleven. A coffee run to Starbucks even though the office had free coffee. I searched for any excuse to get out and about.

It was a strange dilemma. I needed to be left alone to focus on work, but I also didn't want to be alone all the time. I had to find a balance that worked for me.

At the time, my friend Zack was running a startup accelerator in bustling downtown Norfolk. He had secured about 5,000 square feet of free office space from the city and used it to meet with small companies that were starting up or needed business advice. He also had regular meetings with more established companies, and business people dropped by regularly. I was already a mentor to several of the startup founders who were part of his accelerator, and I went to his office about once a week.

He reached out one day and told me that he had an extra room in his office. It was about the same size as the room that I was currently in upstairs in the accountant's office. Since he had free office space from the city, it wouldn't cost me much. Just my fair share for common things like paper towels, toilet paper, and a cleaning person. I also had to pay for a parking garage pass. In total, it'd cost me about $100 a month.

Most of the people who happened into the space were businesspeople. Many were founders of startup companies—ideal prospects for me at the time. He held many business-related learning and social events there too. That meant that I could pop out of my office, walk around the corner to the main area, and bump into someone who may need my services.

More importantly, I could do it quickly without having to drive across town. I could network and save time. Moving in would allow me to save time, money, and build up my network all at once. Seemed like a no-brainer to me.

Shortly after moving in, distractions had once again entered my working hours. Zack and his crew were, let's just say, not as consistently focused on work as I was. Whereas I spent hours working through my clients' problems, their work was more about talking through ideas and meeting with people.

As they'd draw me into a brainstorming session or discussions about the way the world should work, I'd often get sucked in. It was fun, but I also had to get back to my work. So I had to set boundaries. Mostly for myself. I would go into my office and close the door.

If someone walked by and tried to get my attention through the window when I was deep in thought, I'd signal that I was in the middle of something. They'd often keep walking by and find someone else to distract. I was able to find a balance between the social activities of an office space and the quiet that I needed for work.

For downtime, I would attend one of the onsite learning or social events. Pretty quickly, I learned about the struggles of the businesspeople who rolled through the space. Often, I learned that companies were struggling to find new customers.

The need for work would become a common theme with all of the businesses that I bumped into. I'd even occasionally give a talk to the newer entrepreneurs about how I was getting leads. Ironically, giving talks about how I got leads would result in me getting more leads. I also started talking about various business topics, such as what I was learning from starting my company. Those were the early days of sharing my experiences, which are now culminating in this book.

In retrospect, moving into his space was one of the better business decisions I made in those early days. It created relationships that have lasted to this day, and those relationships led to the local work that I needed at the time to augment my online work.

By the time I moved out one and a half years later, almost all my work was coming from the network I built while there. Local projects worked out better for me than my initial online projects. There was less competition for the work and they seemed to run more smoothly.

Local clients also meant that I'd see clients in person. Meeting with people in person, versus communicating over the phone or by email, meant forming stronger, longer-lasting relationships. Those stronger relationships resulted in not only more work from each client, but referrals.

My business grew, and as I hired employees, I began to outgrow the space. When I moved out, I didn't move far. Just across the street. I could walk back to Zack's whenever I wanted and pop in for learning or social events.

For your first office, I recommend that you keep your costs down, find a place where you can focus and where you can have some social interaction. A coworking space is a good option. Usually for about $500 a month, you can rent a dedicated office space with a desk, chair, phone, internet, and lots of internet bandwidth. Coworking spaces also host social and learning functions, often inviting speakers to talk on different business topics.

If you prefer a different type of space, see if any of your business friends have a spare room in their office. Or check out Craigslist like I did. There are a lot of benefits to being close to other businesspeople, as long as you can keep the distractions at bay.

Chapter takeaways

1. An LLC is a common business entity that works great for most businesses.
2. Be sure to pay for and get a business license.
3. Your network is a powerful asset. Activate it by telling the world about your new business.
4. Update all your online profiles to be consistent with your single persona.
5. Build a website so you're perceived as a legitimate business.
6. Opt for business cards that will make you stand out from the crowd.
7. Office space not only provides you and your team with a dedicated place to work, it helps to build your culture. Consider renting a coworking space before growing into a space of your own.

30% → $1M

→ MILLION DOLLAR JOURNEY

→ 07

Getting clients

One of the most frequently asked questions I get is, "How do I get clients?" Although most entrepreneurs want one surefire way, the reality is that it takes several different techniques for you to get and keep your prospects' attention. Here are several techniques I've used successfully for years.

→ Attending events

There are several reasons to attend an event, either in person or online. The first is to learn. The second is to network. Both are important reasons to attend an event, but the most important for you at this point in your entrepreneurial journey is to network.

Although you already have a network, you'll always want to grow it. When you think of your network, don't just consider your first-degree connections—those you know directly. Also consider your second-degree connections—people you don't know, yet, but someone in your network knows.

Why are second-degree connections important? Every person you know, in turn, knows several hundred or even several thousand people. Your first-degree connections can introduce or refer you to their connections! The more people you meet, the bigger your overall network becomes. Make it a habit, especially early-on in your journey, to continuously find new people to network with.

If someone invites you to a networking event, make every effort to go. Networking events are great when you have a "sponsor"—someone who has invited you and can introduce you to other attendees. Having a sponsor is a great opportunity that works to your advantage.

If you're lacking these kinds of warm networking opportunities, then find other networking events to attend. Check out meetup.com and eventbrite.com for events in your area that seem interesting and could have prospects in attendance. It can be awkward to attend a networking event where you don't know anyone, but it's vital that you overcome your angst.

What's the best way to network at one of these mingling events? Simply walk up to someone, look them in the eye, stick out your hand (or offer a fist bump or elbow bump), and say "Hi, my name is …" Resist asking them "What do you do?" It's an awkward question that everyone else asks, and it's typically a dead-end to the conversation.

Instead, prepare a few topics that you can use as icebreakers. Ask them if they attend these meetings often, talk about a current event, or talk about the presentation you are about to see. Just defer asking them "What do you do?" for as long as possible.

When you're talking to people, don't ask them for work! At some point, the conversation will naturally turn toward what you do. Simply tell them what you do, but don't ask if they need your offering.

As an example I usually say something simple like, "I run a digital marketing agency." If it so happens they need what you do, then they will let you know. If they don't, then they won't, and that's okay too. Your goal at this point is simply to make an acquaintance and to add someone to your network. Your goal is not to sell. Not yet, anyway.

When you go back to the same networking event another time, then hopefully you'll see a familiar face or two. Each time you go back, you'll get more comfortable because you'll know more people, and you will know them better than before. It will get less awkward, and eventually they'll all know you and what you do.

When an opportunity arises—when someone they know needs your offering—they'll naturally come to you. The more you stay in front of them, the more top of mind you'll be when opportunities pop up.

→ The art of following up

At each networking event you attend, try to exchange business cards with each person you talk to. Even if you told them your name and your company name, they may quickly forget. A business card helps them to remember. It also gives them your contact information so they can reach out if they, or someone they know, needs your offering one day.

It's too easy, and common, for people to take the business cards they get from networking meetings and simply put them on a shelf to never be looked at again. If you do this, then what was the point of getting business cards in the first place? Instead, you want to put them to use.

Here's what I do with each business card I receive.

- → I add them into my Contacts app. That way I can call on them or text them easily. I make a note in their

- contact record of when and where I met them so that later on my notes will jog my memory.
- → I email or text them the next day, saying that it was great to meet them. If you can recall a tidbit about them or your conversation, then include that in your message.
- → I invite them to join my email list. If you do this, don't add them directly to your list. That will annoy them because they didn't ask to be spammed. Instead, tell them about your newsletter and why you think it's relevant to them, and that they'll get an email from Mailchimp (or whatever system you use) in a minute about joining. If they want to join, they can. If they don't want to join, they can do nothing and stay off your list.
- → If I think they could become a client one day, then I'll make a task for myself to reach out again in a week or two. If I'm going to another networking event, then I'll ask if they're going too. If we're having our own event, then I'll invite them to attend. Even if they don't come, just being invited is flattering. It's also simply an excuse to get back in front of them again.

The important thing is to not do what many people do—send a connection request on LinkedIn and then never contact them again. Use your collected business cards to your advantage by creating a process for adding them to your contacts and following up with them.

→ Hosting your own events

In addition to showing up to someone else's networking event, you can host your own. The great thing about hosting your own events is that all of the goodwill of the event is channeled to you and your company.

Most people think that if they host an event, it'll cost an arm and a leg. It doesn't have to. You can get away with hosting events that aren't that expensive, are relatively easy to put together, and strategically collect people you want to get in front of.

The first event I held was a small happy hour. I invited eight people to join me: a mix of current clients, business acquaintances, and two prospects. We met at a local restaurant known for its wine. I bought a round of appetizers and the first round of drinks. After that, drinks were on the person who ordered them. That was a good way to cap the cost which was, including the tip, $173. The result?

Although I didn't walk away with any signed contracts, it led to relationships that I still tap into to this day. I can call on any of the attendees, ask if they know someone I'm interested in meeting, and if they do, they'll make an introduction.

They'll even proactively send leads my way. A one-time expense of $173 is an inexpensive way to establish a tight network of referral partners. But you can't stop at just one of these events.

The next event I hosted was at my first office. I had moved into that office about six months earlier and a grand opening was overdue. I wanted to keep costs down, so I skipped the caterer and did it myself. We ordered and picked up trays of shrimp, cheeses, fruit, and other finger food that could be put on the conference room table without much preparation or fuss during the event. An assortment of beer and wine topped off the offering.

I sent out invitations which included the phrase, "*We've invited mostly business owners and managers of companies we work with.*" I included this sentence so those invited would recognize the valuable network in attendance and realize it would be worth their time. I wasn't just inviting people to some random event. I was inviting them to mingle with my clients. The implication was that my clients could become their clients. That was something of value.

I also included, "*Feel free to bring someone else who you think would be a good fit for us to work with.*" This turned out to be a $20,000 sentence.

The wording in that last sentence was important. I didn't want them to bring a co-worker, friend, or date. What I wanted, and what I requested, was to bring someone who could possibly become one of my clients.

One person I invited ended up inviting one of her clients to join her. She even brought him to my office early so we could talk before the event. Turned out he had a business idea which required a new website, which was exactly the type of work we did!

He didn't even stay for the event because he had a conflict. But he returned a couple of days later to continue the conversation. That quickly led to a signed contract for $20,000 of new work.

The event cost me about $1,000. In addition to the tangible return on investment of $20,000 in new work, we created a ton of good will, strengthened connections with other business owners in the community, and generated a few additional leads. The event was a winner. Things were working out so well with event hosting that I started to take it up a notch.

A month later, I co-hosted an event at our local minor league baseball field. Splitting a suite three ways with two other business owners, we each invited five guests to join us for opening night of the season. Each guest was a business owner. It was a great room to be in, and it was an excellent event to host, but nothing materialized out of it for me. It felt a bit too swanky for me.

I decided to go big on the next one. I rented a sailboat for my next happy hour. Problem was, I was having a difficult time coming up with names of prospects to invite, so most of the attendees ended up being business people I already knew. I spent about $3,000 on the event, which included an open bar. It was cool, but no new leads came out of it.

With the lackluster results from the last two events I threw, I cut back on events. Instead of hosting lavish events, I went back to what worked—inexpensive happy hours in my office. That's where I got the biggest bang for the buck.

I also scaled back on the frequency, hosting happy hours at the office once every six months or so. That felt like the right frequency and provided a good enough return on investment to justify the events and keep new prospects coming in the door.

When throwing your own networking events, think of the business rationale for spending the time and money on them. To keep the costs down, consider holding your events at your office or at a place that will be inexpensive for you. The goal is to provide value to your guests, to meet new prospects, and to generate leads. Not to throw a cool party.

→ Email newsletters

Even if you just have a small list of subscribers to start, email newsletters are a great way to stay in front of prospects, to present you or your company as an expert in the field, and to provide valuable content.

The idea is that someone can sign up for your newsletter, and you'll send them helpful tidbits of news and information. Newsletter content should be related to the offering your company provides, and will allow you to go deeper into a subject than you can on social media. People will subscribe if they are interested in what you have to say and if they perceive that you offer value without a hard sales pitch.

Newsletters are ideal for people who had previously expressed interest in working with you, but either weren't ready to hire you at the time or simply went cold for some reason. They're also good for warming up new prospects who may be interested in working with you soon.

We've experimented with sending out newsletters at different frequencies. At first, we sent them out at random times, essentially when we got around to it. That's a mistake. When you don't give yourself a firm timeline, then that thing that you know you "should do" will always get pushed off. If you're going to send a newsletter, then commit to a regular schedule.

How often should you send your email newsletter?

Some successful email marketers send emails daily. I've never done that because it sounds like a full-time job creating all that content day in and day out. It's also a full-time job as a recipient. When I've been on the receiving end of daily emails, I'll read them for a few days but inevitably unsubscribe in about a week. Daily emails just aren't for me, and probably won't be for you, unless your plan is to directly generate money from your newsletter.

The most common frequency that businesses send newsletters, after "whenever we get around to it," is monthly. Monthly is good for most businesses, most of the time. It's a nice balance between the work it takes to produce the newsletter and the value it provides. It's not too much on anyone, and sending monthly is a good frequency to remind people that you exist.

But sending monthly really isn't frequent enough. A month is a long time for your prospects and customers to have not heard from you. So we've settled on every two weeks, which seems like a good balance between the work it takes to create a newsletter and the value to our recipients.

Here's the important point about frequency—pick a frequency and stick to it. Fully commit to sending your newsletters when you say you'll send them. If you're not sure of the frequency you want for your newsletter, then start with monthly. It's a good compromise.

But what will you say in your newsletters?

The golden rule in newsletters is to provide valuable information. For us, each newsletter is packed with the latest information on digital marketing, with links to our videos, podcast episodes, and articles.

Those articles that are on your website? Include an abstract in your newsletter and link to the full article. Encourage people to click through to your site to read more.

Your social media posts? Find the one that got the most engagement since you sent the last newsletter and feature it as an ICYMI (In Case You Missed It).

If you shoot video, include an image and link it to the full video.

If you host your own events, talk about them in your newsletter. You can include a summary of the last event you held to show subscribers what they missed, and you can tease the next event you'll be holding.

If you find yourself without the time, resources, or energy to create content, then you can forward industry news instead. Select two or three news articles that are pertinent to the work you do, and compile them into your own newsletter.

Last but not least, since you're giving so much valuable information in your newsletter, don't be afraid to include an ask. Your call to action can be for subscribers to attend one of your events, to forward the newsletter to a friend, or to call you if they need your services.

By now you should have an idea of when to send your newsletter, as well as what to say in it. But how do you get subscribers?

We've found that asking people to subscribe to our newsletter on our website didn't result in a lot of sign-ups. Even explaining the value in great detail resulted in few sign-ups.

A different approach is to not ask them to join your newsletter, but instead give them something of value immediately. We've done this by providing a free eBook that we wrote. Once they provide their email address, they can download the eBook. They're told they'll be subscribed to our newsletter, which contains more up-to-date information than could be included in the eBook when it was written. When doing this, be clear that the person is not only getting the eBook, they are also signing up for your list. This technique has led to a tremendous amount of growth in our newsletter audience compared to before.

Instead of waiting for your next newsletter before reaching out to new subscribers, send them a series of initial emails. These initial emails are referred to as a drip campaign.

Your first email in this drip campaign can include a link to your eBook or whatever you're offering at the time.

One problem with email newsletters is that sometimes they get flagged as spam by email providers. To ensure this doesn't happen to ours, we send the link again in our second email and ask the person to email us back to confirm they got the eBook we promised them. Doing so will signal to their email provider that they're interested in what we have to say, and their email provider is more likely to deliver our emails into their inbox in the future.

→ Social media

Most entrepreneurs know they need a presence on social media. Social media is where people hang out these days, and you need to be there too.

It's a weird world out there to the uninitiated. It can be a confusing place no matter what, but especially when promoting your company.

But since people spend so much time these days on social media, it's important to have a solid presence there. When people are online, they're likely on social media, and you need to be there too. Being on social media is important enough that many companies constantly promote their profiles and pages at every opportunity. In print ads. On the sides of their vehicles. They even put social media icons at the top of their homepage, trying to entice people to "follow us." That's a big mistake.

Through advertising, marketing, and a whole lot of hustle, you've worked hard to get people to come to your website. The last thing you want to do after finally getting someone there is to immediately trigger their social media FOMO—fear of missing out—by reminding them to get off of your website and go see what's happened in the last five minutes since they were on social media!

When they see those icons, they're likely to click over. Yes, they'll end up on your profile or page, and there is a chance that they'll follow you. But more likely than not, social media will do its job and provide a never-ending feed of posts from their friends, family, and others they follow. Although you hoped they'd follow you, they'll get sucked into the vortex of social media consumption.

Should you put social media icons on your website? Yes, but at least don't remind them about social media as soon as they land on your site. Instead, put the links at the bottom of your website, in the footer. If someone gets through your entire webpage and still longs to know more about you on social media, then you want to make it easy for them to find you there.

As a goal, instead of sending people from your website to social media, you want to send them from social media to your website. Your website is the place you want all prospects to visit because that is a place you control and a place where you can properly describe your offering in a way that can entice them to contact you.

When creating company content on social media, provide something of value to potential customers. Different social media platforms have different purposes. Some platforms focus on keeping up with your friends. Others focus on keeping up with business contacts. Each is different, and it'll be up to you to figure out which platforms you support.

Some gurus will tell you to be omnipresent—a fancy word for saying that you should be everywhere. The problem is that it'll take hours of your time, every day, to be everywhere. You will need to either devote the vast majority of your time to supporting social media, or you'll need to hire someone to do it for you. It can be worth it, but it's a big investment in time and money and may not have the immediate return on investment that gurus claim.

Before you start creating a presence on all the platforms and then abandoning them due to lack of time and resources, instead think about what you want to say and who you want to say it to. Like writing a newsletter on a regular basis, posting on social media can become a chore. Since it's work to figure out what to post, how to say it, and when to say it, I suggest that you don't put too much effort into social media when you're just starting your company.

Yes, I know that's an odd recommendation from a digital marketer like myself. But I'm also a business owner. Getting work that pays is more important than getting likes when your business is young. Likes, comments, and social media are cool and may make you feel good, but they don't pay the bills. It takes an awful lot of work on social media to generate leads.

So for now, do yourself a favor and mostly skip social media and focus on what really counts—sourcing new customers from your network and doing awesome work. But when you're ready, come back to social media with a vengeance.

When it's time for you to start playing the social media game, you'll need to make a few decisions.

First, which social media platforms will you support?

If you're a B2B company, meaning your business sells to other businesses, then concentrate on social media platforms built for business relationships. As of the time of this writing, LinkedIn is the dominant social media for business relationships.

If you're a B2C company, meaning your business sells to individual consumers, then you'll want to support social media platforms where people aren't there for business; they're there for pleasure. Right now, Facebook and Instagram are where it's at, but there are new challengers on a monthly basis.

For starters, pick just one social media platform and support it fully. When you get more advanced, once your company is humming, you will want to support more social media platforms.

Once you've selected the social media platform that's most important to you, what are you going to do on it? After adding your obligatory profile pictures and basic data, it'll be time to publish a few posts.

I recommend you pick a posting schedule that you can commit to. Social media gurus often recommend posting multiple times a day. Posts, stories, videos, going live—if you want to be on social media almost nonstop, then social media has the ability to support that. But let's face facts—you're not ready for all that yet. The reality is that you're just now standing up your business, and you have too much on your plate already. You cannot afford to spend too much of your finite time on social media. You need to stay focused on getting work and delivering for your clients.

Social media is a perk. You want to be there, but you can only do so much. Do it, but don't overdo it.

I recommend you post at least three times a week. If you're writing an email newsletter, then you can and should recycle a lot of that content into social media posts. If you've written an article for your website, then you can break down that article into multiple individual posts. Perhaps copy a sentence or two from the article, and paste that in your social media post. Include an applicable image (people love to see other people on social media). Occasionally include a link back to the full article on your website. But don't always include a link because social media algorithms don't favor posts that try to get people to leave their platform.

If you're sharing industry news in your newsletter, then you can do the same on social media. Just be sure to share content that your prospects will find interesting. Social media, like all other company messaging, should target your ideal clients only, even to the detriment of others like your friends and family. Remember, you're after clients, not to entertain your friends and family who very likely will never buy from you! But most importantly, what you post should be pertinent to your business. These posts should remind people of what you do and why that's important to them.

When someone comments on your post, reply to them. In your spare time, which I know feels less abundant with every passing day, look at some of your followers' posts and drop a comment on them. Comments are powerful ways to interact. Comments show that you're interested in the topic at hand, which should be relevant to your business, and exposes you to your followers' audience.

Comments are also a much better option than simply liking a post. With a comment, you are contributing to an ongoing conversation and engaging with a person. Comments take more time to provide than a like, get you more exposure than a like, and are rewarded much more by social media algorithms. Even better, do both and like and comment on posts!

When posting, show your personality and have fun. Remember, people are on social media to escape the pressures of life. So have fun.

All that said, you're on social media because you want something out of social media for your business. In the end, you need to extract some value; otherwise, how could it be good for business?

Although you want to extract some value from your social media activity, you should be cautious to not publish too many salesy posts. Nothing is more annoying than following a company, or a person who runs a company, and they're always selling something on social media. People aren't there to be sold to, but they are open to the occasional sales pitch if done correctly. Sell infrequently and only after giving tips, tricks, and generally adding value to the platform. As a basic rule, never sell in more than one out of every ten posts.

One more thing about social media—there's real power in direct messages (aka DMs). Whenever I get a new connection, I always send them a DM basically saying what I would say in the real world. Something like, *Hi, my name is Erik. I run a marketing agency. How are you*?

It's simple but highly effective. Few people do this on social media. When most people get a new connection, they never interact with that person. That's a mistake. Take a few seconds to DM each new connection and say hi, and you'll set yourself miles apart from what your lazy competitors are doing. Or more accurately, what they're not doing.

→ Referrals

As you continue to market yourself, and more people who you know start to realize the type of work that you do, they will come across opportunities that may be a fit for you.

Referrals are a great source of work because a potential client has been recommended to you by someone they trust. Because they trust the person who referred them to you, they immediately place a level of trust in you before they ever contact you. I've found that a high percentage of referrals to me, assuming they are a good fit, become clients. The best kinds of new projects and clients come from referrals, and you want as many of those as possible.

Since referrals are such a great source of new work, it's in your best interest to continually ask people you know for referrals. This serves a few purposes.

For starters, by asking them if they know anyone who may be a fit for your work, you are indirectly asking them for their business. You're not coming right out and saying it, but since you're asking for anyone who you could work with, they could very likely think of themselves. This is a safe way to ask someone for their business without being so blunt and awkward about it.

It's also an opportunity for you to remind your network about what you do. Often your request for a referral will lead someone who already knows you to ask for clarification on "exactly" what you do. It happens to me all the time.

When someone asks for clarification, be sure to summarize what you do in a simple manner. Now is not the time to start geeking out and throwing technobabble jargon at them. Remember, you need to communicate simply because they have to carry that message forward to others. All too often when I meet new entrepreneurs and ask what they do, they answer, but I'm no closer to understanding what they actually do. Be clear and simple in your answer.

→ Referral fees

Some people will only refer work to you if they get a referral fee. This is a common request when you are a one-person show. The concept is that someone will introduce a connection to you, and if you land the work, you will pay the referring person a fee. After all, you wouldn't have the work unless your "friend" made the introduction, right?

The fee could be a one-time fee or could be a percentage of the revenue you generate as a result of the introduction. I've had people ask me for referral fees of as high as 20 percent!

About a year into my business, an acquaintance—someone who owned a slightly similar business to mine—had a client who needed more specialized work than he could provide. He brought the opportunity to me and requested a 10 percent fee of the project revenue. At the time I was worried about not having enough work and was thankful to get the lead, so I agreed to the terms.

He introduced me to his client, and I took it from there. I had several meetings with the client, developed the scope of work, proposed a solution, negotiated the terms, and started working. As I got paid, I'd pay my friend who referred me his 10 percent. The project continued on for months, almost a year, and I continued to make his referral payments. But as time marched on, I started to regret the deal.

Here I was busting my butt day in and day out, and he wasn't doing a thing on the project. I was 100 percent responsible for the work—I had to do the work, deliver the work, deal with the client, and nag the client for payment. My referral partner didn't have any responsibility after making the introduction. It just didn't seem fair that I continued to pay him when I was the one with all of the ongoing responsibility, work, and liability. Even though I wasn't thrilled about it, I continued with the deal, but it left a bad taste in my mouth.

Another time, I was approached by another business owner for another referral. They knew someone who they thought may need my assistance. I again agreed to a 10 percent referral fee for the lead. But this time the referral partner didn't exactly hand me the project on a silver platter. Instead he forwarded me an email where the potential prospect had mentioned possibly having a need.

When I reached out to the person to see if they wanted to work with me, it was extremely awkward. He had never mentioned to anyone that he actually wanted someone with my abilities, and I was contacting him out of the blue. I didn't get the deal, but I did learn a lesson from all this—I realized that I had certain expectations on how these referral partnerships should work going forward.

I tried structuring future referral fee deals so that the referring person had some responsibility in the deal. After all, if they were going to get paid, then I figured I should get something in return besides just an intro.

On one project, I made the person who referred the deal to me the project manager. He was supposed to communicate with the customer on my behalf. This seemed great—I'd get the project, pay the same referral fee as normal, but now I'd have less work to do because the referral partner would manage the project. Win/win.

But it turned into a huge disaster. He wasn't exactly the project management type and didn't know a thing about what I was doing on the project. He just wasn't involved enough to know what was going on. I had to spoon-feed him what to say, and he blundered the message enough times that I had to jump in and take over project management. That was the last time I tried to involve a third party in my projects.

After trying many less-than-successful referral partnerships, I finally came up with an arrangement which worked well for me and the referring partners. Here's what I would need from them.

First, the referring partner would need to provide a warm introduction. What I needed was more of an endorsement than just an intro or forwarding an email. Something like, "I'd like to introduce you to Erik. He does great work and I recommend him." These kinds of endorsements worked great to warm up a cold lead.

Next, I set the expectation that my referral partner wouldn't have any responsibility on the project. I would take care of everything. If they insisted on being involved, then I'd tell them that we had a process which allowed them to get their referral fee without them having to do any additional work.

Third, I needed to have a direct relationship with the client. Being a subcontractor to your referral partner so that your money and communications flow through them ... it's just not a good situation. You want to have as close of a relationship with the end client as possible. Otherwise you're just a commodity.

By the way, if someone offers to get you work from their client, but they won't tell you who the client is or let you talk to the client, just walk away. Every time I've entered into a project like that, it was a disaster. Don't even waste your time trying to scope a project and negotiate with a third party—it's always been a total waste of my time. You must have a relationship with the client. If you cannot even talk to the client and must go through an intermediary, then the project is doomed to fail because the intermediary cannot communicate the project needs like you can. Trust me on this one. These kinds of "leads" always turn into nightmare scenarios.

Lastly, the referral fee would be capped to a maximum amount. I started agreeing to provide 10 percent of the revenue of a project to the person who referred me, but I'd limit the total payments to a certain amount. The amount has varied over time, but $500 to $1,000 was about where I landed on the maximum referral fees paid for a project.

Sure, someone could argue that if I got a $100,000 project, then $1,000 wasn't enough of a cut. But think about all of the work that I would have to do to get that $100,000. I'd have to turn the prospect into a client, define the project, write up the contract, do the work, manage my team, deliver the work, warranty the work, literally insure the work, and chase down the client until they paid me. I had significant payroll and other expenses. But on their end, they simply had to send an email intro and they were done. Come on! Fair is fair, and a $1,000 referral fee is more than fair!

Referrals are great and you'll always want referral work. But referral fees suck. As you're getting started, though, they are worth the investment. Otherwise, you may starve because you just don't have the mechanism or brand built up enough for people to know about you and seek you out directly. So pay the referral fees, but do it on your terms. Write down your terms for giving referral fees, and make sure that your referral partners know what to expect before they send work your way.

Speaking of which, you will have situations when people send work your way, don't mention that they want a referral fee, but then request a referral fee after you land the work. This has happened to me on multiple occasions. Each time, it has been frustrating for me because I didn't realize the person who made the referral had wanted a referral fee, and then when it was sprung on me, my profits would decrease.

The first time or two this happened, I played ball, gave in, and paid a retroactive referral fee. But I felt suckered and never appreciated the surprise. I also didn't appreciate my referral partner making me feel like I owed them or had wronged them for not paying a referral fee that was not even requested, never mind agreed to.

Once I wrote my referral policy down, when someone attempted to retroactively hit me up, I was in a better position to defend myself. I'd tell them that I'd be happy to work with them on future projects and would send them my referral policy.

That document included a statement that all referral fees must be agreed upon before the introduction to the prospect is made. I'd tell them that if I had known about their desire for a referral fee upfront, then I could have priced it into the contract. But since they didn't tell me, I hadn't priced it in and it was too late. I couldn't go back to the client now and raise my price by 10 percent!

→ Advertising

Knowing I needed to get my name out to more people than my network, I reached out to a saleswoman at the local business journal to talk about running print advertisements. The publication is 100 percent focused on business stories, business events, and the movers and shakers in the local business community. Reading that journal was ideal for me for many years and is how I began to understand where the power in the business world resides.

When it came to advertising to business owners, the local business journal seemed like the ideal place to advertise. She recommended that I run a one-fourth-page color ad in the paper every other week. In addition, they were coming out with a quarterly print magazine that she assured me would be a huge hit.

I agreed to a one-year deal that would eventually cost me $10,000. After I signed up, she mentioned, almost in passing, that this first round of advertising was more for creating brand awareness than for lead generation. In retrospect, that statement, more like a warning, was significant.

It was exciting the first time I saw my ad in the journal. I thought that I had finally made it! But as the months went on and I saw my ad more often, I realized that no one was mentioning it to me. My phone wasn't ringing more, we didn't get more website form submissions, and I couldn't trace a single prospect back to the ad. In fact, in the whole year that the ad ran, only one person mentioned the ad to me, and it was someone I already knew who couldn't afford my services. He simply stated that he saw the ad and wanted me to know.

That's it! One guy mentioned he saw the ad, and it cost me ten grand! Needless to say, I did not renew with them. Even with that terrible return on investment, I didn't give up on advertising.

Next, I shifted to online advertising. Being into Twitter for a number of years, that seemed like the next place to try advertising. I ran a couple of ads that targeted people who followed relevant accounts, like the Chamber of Commerce and other business organizations in my area.

At about one hundred dollars a week, I was spending half of what I had spent in the paper. I got a lot of eyeballs on the ads, but they weren't doing anything to draw in work. At least that's what I thought until one day I received the following email:

> I am interested in hiring your company to make me a clone of [XYZ]. I currently run an educational site but I have to use their software to host my quizzes. I am looking to run it on my own server and add some features such as PayPal integration to allow instant access, add a feature to restrict users to only one active session at any given time, and a few other features. Can we set up a meeting?

Turns out he saw our Twitter ad several times before deciding to contact me. That one lead turned into hundreds of thousands of dollars of work spread out over three years.

He was a great client, the project was interesting, and the revenue from it allowed us to staff up. That additional staff later allowed us to win other work from other clients. It turned into a snowball effect that would push us closer to the coveted $1 million per year mark.

In retrospect, now that I know a whole lot more about advertising, I'm not surprised at my early results (or lack of results) with advertising. The paper was a lousy place for us to advertise, as is any broadcast media. The problem is that it's completely untargeted and sprays your message randomly to anyone with a pulse.

Advertising online is a much better investment of your limited funds. With online advertising, you can target people ready to buy, at the moment they have an intent, with search ads or by narrowing your audience down granularly with social media posts.

Figure out who may be interested in your offering, where they hang out online, and then advertise there. Target them directly, and craft a message so they think you're speaking directly to them.

Advertising is an investment. Set aside a small amount at first, even just five dollars a day. You'll get better results over time as you learn the advertising platforms. One day, you'll likely land that huge gig like I did!

Chapter takeaways

1. Always work on growing your network.
2. If someone invites you to a networking event, make every attempt to go.
3. Email or text new contacts the day after you meet them. Tell them it was nice to meet them. If you think they could become a client one day, then find a reason to reach out within a week.
4. Hosting your own events is the best way to network. It doesn't have to be expensive. Consider hosting happy hours with clients and prospects at your office.
5. Get in the routine of emailing value-packed newsletters on a regular basis. It'll remind prospects and referral partners of your offering and will give you plenty of content to use for other purposes.
6. Turn newsletter content and articles you create into micro-content to be shared regularly on your social media channels. Always respond to comments and engage with your followers by commenting on their posts on a regular basis.
7. Referrals are a great source of new business. Encourage your current clients and others to recommend someone they know who would make a good client for you.

8. Protect yourself from excessive referral fees. Document your referral fee policy and only pay for referrals that follow your policy. Cap the total amount you'll pay for a referral to ensure you don't keep paying long after the introduction was made.
9. Like most businesses, you'll want to advertise to find new clients. Select advertising opportunities where you can very narrowly target your ideal prospect. Avoid broadcast advertising and opt for online advertising instead.

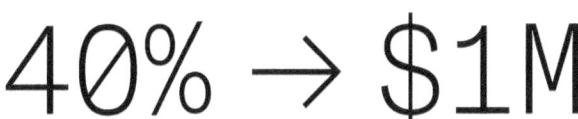

40% → $1M

→ MILLION DOLLAR JOURNEY

→ 08

Getting paid

Most of us start our own businesses for one of two reasons.

Some have a burning desire to work on their own terms and aren't too interested in business matters unless it impacts their ability to create. Others may have that passion, too, but are in it primarily to earn a living or grow an empire. Regardless of the reason, in the end you have to get paid for your work.

Asking to get paid can feel like an awkward conversation for most new entrepreneurs. They're proud of their work, but it seems aggressive or even taboo to ask to get fairly compensated. It shouldn't be this way, and it doesn't have to. You're doing great work, and that work brings inherent value. Make sure you get paid for the value you provide.

But unfortunately, getting paid is not straightforward at all. It's complex, and much of getting paid rests on the expectations you establish at the onset of working with a client. Here we'll review several different ways you can charge for your work, along with the pros and cons of each.

→ Billing by the hour

Almost all entrepreneurs who provide a service start off charging by the hour. This is the default billing mechanism for so many because it's easy for the entrepreneur.

When you're new at something, when it's one of your first projects, you simply don't know how much time it's going to take you. Sure, you can guess how long it'll take, but you also realize that you want to get paid for your work even if it ends up taking longer than you guessed. You equate money to time. Likely, your previous jobs paid you by the hour so it seems natural to you.

Getting paid by the hour works fine when you're a freelancer doing work on the side to make extra money. The short-term predictability of the model is enticing, too—you know that if you put in four hours and charge, say, $50/hour, then you'll make $200. That's easy to understand and may seem like a win/win to you early in your journey. But there are problems with this model that you'll uncover as you take on more clients.

Part of the problem with billing by the hour is that you're working for time. If you don't put in the time, you don't make the money. So although you can make good money working by the hour, you're capped by your hours.

Worse, you have to keep putting in the time. There's no scaling your time. Time literally equals money. There's no opportunity to separate the two, so you have to keep slaving away or you can't bill. There are no efficiencies.

A second problem with working by the hour is that you can't invoice your customer until after you've put in the time. After all, you don't know how much time a project will take, so you can't invoice them accurately until after the work is done. For longer projects, you'll likely agree to bill them every week or two, but you can't predict how many hours you'll burn through in that time.

Since you're billing after the fact, also known as "in arrears," you're having to wait to receive payment for the work you've already done. There's a lag between when you work—when you provide value—and when you can reap the reward for the value you provided. The longer that delay, the more of a cash flow problem you create.

As a one-person freelancing shop, that lag is not a big deal. After all, freelancing provides newfound money, so what's the difference if you get paid upfront or in arrears? As long as the client doesn't stiff you, that is.

But once you have an employee or two, or ten, the model becomes much harder to sustain. Employees like to get paid on a regular basis, regardless of when you get paid. Since you're billing in arrears, that means you'll end up paying your employees before you get paid by your client. Since you're fronting the money for your employees to work on your client's project, you are literally funding your client's work. You are also taking all of the financial risk. Sometimes a client just won't pay, and that means the money you paid your employees to work on the client project is for naught.

Another big problem with billing by the hour is that you're not charging for the value you provide, only for the time it takes to create it. Sometimes there can be a big difference between the time value of the work it takes to create something and the value that it provides the client.

Imagine if you put in a week's worth of work, forty hours, into solving a problem. If you bill at one hundred dollars an hour, then you'll get paid $4,000. Sounds great, right? But what if your work results in your client making or saving $10,000 a month? If they will continue to realize that value month after month, then their value from your work is $120,000 a year.

If your client can make $120,000 in a year, then do you think they'd be willing to pay more than $4,000 for the solution? Of course, you want to provide great value to your client, and they need to profit from your work, but you left a lot on the table. Had you priced the work differently, you'd likely be able to charge more for that exact same work. Maybe twice as much. Maybe more.

Does paying $8,000 for a $120,000 return sound like a good deal to you? It does to me. How about paying $12,000 for a $120,000 return? That still is a great value. It's possible that you could charge two to three times more for your work if you priced your work differently.

When you bill by the hour, you're pegging your pay to time and labor instead of the value you provide. By doing that, you've turned yourself into a commodity. The goal of buying a commodity is to buy it for as little as possible. By pricing by the hour, you're almost begging prospects to compare your hourly rate to the hourly rate of others. Most often they'll pick the cheapest. Sure, you can try to convince them that you provide superior work, excellent craftsmanship, blah blah blah, but everyone else is making the same promises too.

A final problem with billing by the hour is that clients generally hate it because there's uncertainty. When a client hires you by the hour, they don't like the fact that they don't know how many hours it'll take you to complete the job. Shoot, you don't even know.

They likely have a final budget in mind, that you probably don't know about, and they've calculated how many hours, based on your rate, they're willing to pay you to complete the project. That number will likely not match with the number of hours you're thinking it will take to finish the project, if you even have an idea at all, and likely will not match what it will actually take.

None of this, by the way, is typically communicated between you and your client because you're both predicting the final cost of the project. It's in their best interest for you to put in as little time as possible to keep the cost down. But it's in your best interest, honestly, to put in more time to maximize what you get paid.

So although you're billing by the hour, the client has done the math and is thinking in terms of overall budget. You may have agreed on an hourly rate, but their objective is to limit their financial risk and pay less rather than more. To achieve this objective, you'll find that they'll not only want an hourly rate, but they'll also want you to commit to the number of hours it'll take. And that's when the hourly model breaks down.

Once you give an estimate for the number of hours a project will take, you've committed yourself to that estimate. By doing so, you've essentially committed to a fixed price project where the maximum you can charge is set by your hourly rate and the number of hours you said it'd take. But you also could be paid less for the same work if it ends up taking less time. In effect, you've committed to covering the risk of overages while "giving back" money if the project goes faster than expected. From your perspective, there's more risk and, at the same time, less reward. That's the worst of both worlds for you.

If you finish in fewer hours than expected, then you'll get paid less than the overall estimate. If you finish in more hours than expected, then you'll get paid your hourly rate times the original estimate of hours. If you try to go back after the project and tell the client it actually took you more hours to complete the project than you estimated, you'll be in for a fight. They'll exert extreme pressure for you to "honor" your estimated number of hours. Believe it or not, you'll feel compelled to bill for fewer hours than it actually took you in order to either avoid that fight or to appease your client. So even though you told them you want to get paid by the hour, you end up sort of working by the hour and sort of working like a fixed price project.

I've done this on numerous occasions. When I was billing by the hour, and if I knew my client's final budget, I'd invoice for fewer hours than it took me in order to fit into their budget. As an example, if a project took me forty hours to complete but the client could only afford thirty-two hours at my hourly rate, then I'd only bill for thirty-two hours.

Every time I did that, I'd make an excuse to myself for why I undercharged. Perhaps I had to do some research and I didn't charge for that. Or I didn't charge for meetings. Or I justified not charging the client for the time it took to answer their questions or to create the reports they requested. Or some similar excuse. Talk to any freelancer who bills by the hour, and you'll hear excuses like these. It's much easier to justify why you're not charging by the hour, like you said you would, than to try to bill for all of the time you put into a project when you knew the client was capped at a total project cost.

Avoid falling into the trap of wanting to satisfy your client, which means meeting their budget, even if that means not billing for all of your hours. If the client actually has a fixed price, then you should consider a fixed price budget instead.

→ Fixed price projects

Charging by the project, or fixed price projects, is a big step up from charging by the hour.

A fixed price project means that when a prospect asks you for a price, instead of quoting your hourly rate and the number of hours it should take, you instead quote a total price for the whole project.

With a fixed price quote, clients know exactly how much the project is going to cost them. They no longer need to worry about your hourly rate or how many hours you will bill them before the job is completed. They no longer need to worry about whether you'll hit an unexpected snag that'll cost them more time and thus money. All they need to worry about is whether you produced what they think they asked you to produce. Note: "think" is a critical word here, which I'll come back to in a minute.

With an hourly agreement, you don't agree to produce a defined scope of work—you just agree that you have the skills needed to work on their project, and that you'll work on their project for as long as it's mutually agreeable. But with a fixed price contract, you've agreed to produce the defined scope of work and at a set price.

The reason that clients feel comfortable with fixed price projects is because they've shifted a lot of the risk of the project over to you. In particular, and in the client's mind, it doesn't matter if it takes you 20 percent longer or 100 percent longer to do the work than you thought it would take, because they didn't agree to pay you by the hour.

So if a fixed price project shifts the risk to you, why would you want to take on a fixed price project?

For starters, clients love this kind of arrangement. If you propose to do a job for a fixed price, and your competitor proposed to do it by the hour, then you'll likely have the upper hand. With hourly work, there's always contractual wiggle room for someone to charge more than the client thought they would be charged.

The second big reason you'd want to propose a fixed price project is because once you've become efficient at the kind of work you do, you'll know that you can do it much faster than others and avoid common pitfalls they'll likely fall into. If you can do a project faster than your competitors, then there's an opportunity for you to charge about the same, or maybe a little less, and make a nice margin!

So let's say you want to bid your next project at a fixed price. How much should you charge? No matter what, you'll want to make more than your normal hourly rates since you're taking on risk. But how much more?

Well, with fixed cost projects the real question is: How much value will you produce for the client?

My first foray into fixed price projects was on a maintenance contract. I had built a database project for a physical therapy company in Southern California. The client was happy with the results from that first project, but an intermittent connectivity issue kept affecting what I had built.

My client had an IT company on retainer, and I asked them to monitor the scheduled jobs to see if the connectivity issues were affecting us. If so, I gave them instructions to re-run the job. Once a week or two, I'd log in and notice that the jobs had failed. I would re-run the jobs myself and remind my client and the IT company that I would like them to monitor for failures. But my request went unanswered, and I kept finding that the IT company didn't monitor the jobs like I'd requested multiple times. Realizing that their failure to monitor was making me look bad, I decided that we'd monitor the jobs if they wouldn't.

I asked Katya, my assistant at the time, to check on the jobs three times a week. If the job had failed, she'd let me know, and I'd log in, get it running again, and bill them for my time to fix it. She also billed for her time to check the job.

When I realized she was only charging five minutes each time she logged in to check, and that we were charging pennies on the dollar for the monitoring that the IT company would charge much more for, I asked Katya to bill a minimum of fifteen minutes each time.

Knowing Katya's billable rate at the time, and one quarter of an hour of that rate, felt like an appropriate price. After all, the client was getting value out of us discovering that the job failed, so we could fix it fast, and they should pay for monitoring the job.

I further rationalized her charging more time than it actually took in order to account for "context shifting"—the justification that by-the-hour people use to charge more than it actually takes to do small amounts of work. Context shifting is a fancy way of saying that when you switch from one task to another, it takes your brain a certain amount of time to get into the "flow" … to re-remember the task at hand and where you were before shifting to some other task.

With that rationalization, many by-the-hour people create rules for themselves that they'll charge a minimum of a half hour, or some amount of minimal time, regardless of how long it actually takes them to do the work. What this amounts to is a game where they want the ease of charging by the hour, but also want the reward of charging for value.

Even with that rationalization, neither Katya nor I felt comfortable billing for more time than was actually put in. After talking about it, we decided to charge a fixed amount on a monthly basis. The amount that we charged was much more than the amount we would have otherwise charged if we simply billed five minutes each time she checked the job. Here's how.

Her billable rate was forty-five dollars an hour. At five minutes per check, three times a week and four weeks per month, we'd only bill for one hour and make forty-five dollars in a month if we had charged by the hour. But since we were billing as a fixed price project, and realizing that forty-five dollars just wasn't worth it for us to take on the liability of doing the work that the IT company should have been doing, I decided we had to charge more. But how much more?

First, I thought about how much the IT company would charge to do that same work. Certainly, it'd be in the hundreds of dollars per month. Second, I understood that when those jobs failed, it caused all sorts of problems for the company and required hours of work by their staff to reconcile the data issues. By monitoring the jobs, we could catch those issues before they became bigger, more expensive problems.

How much would my client pay to avoid their staff having to spend hours to fix the data issues? I thought $300 per month was certainly much less than the cost of the problems that could be avoided. Was that a rip-off?

I didn't think so at all, and neither did my client. Actually, they were quite relieved that we would ensure the jobs ran smoothly.

That's a perfect example of when it makes sense to bill by the project instead of by the hour. When you expect to be efficient, so efficient that the amount of time you spend multiplied by your hourly rate is less than the value you deliver, you should bill as a fixed price project. But there's a caveat, and it's all about scoping.

By scoping, I mean enumerating the scope of work—describing exactly what you'll deliver with the project. Since you're agreeing to a fixed price for a fixed scope of work, if you don't take the time to fully understand everything in the scope, but agree to deliver it, then you're still on the hook for it. What often happens with new entrepreneurs is they don't understand exactly what "it" is that they're agreeing to deliver.

You, and only you, are responsible for defining the scope of work to ensure you know what you're agreeing to! You have to define "it," the thing you're delivering, because your client likely doesn't even have a full grasp of what exactly "it" is. They likely have a vision, and a foggy one at that, but it's up to you to clarify what's in and out of the vision they've conveyed to you.

This will require a varying degree of upfront work on your part to fully understand their vision, take whatever scope of work they give you, and fully define the scope of work that you are proposing to deliver. You may have to do some research into how exactly you can pull off what they're asking you to do. It's time-consuming to fully flesh out the scope of work, but always, always propose your own scope of work. Do not simply agree to what they give you because it will likely have lots of holes in it.

All of that research into the scope, and all of the time and effort and conversations with the potential client to define the scope, is traditionally not billable time when you propose a fixed price project. That means that you'll often provide this type of consulting to a client without getting paid. Many times, you'll do this work and provide the scope and pricing, and the prospective client ends up not accepting your proposal. Each time that happens, you've wasted your time and potentially a ton of it.

That's not the case with a by-the-hour contract. You typically spend little time upfront trying to anticipate the pitfalls in the scope because you're not on the clock yet. A glance at the requested scope is typically enough to realize if there are any big problems and to determine if there's a fit for you. But with fixed price projects, you have to be more prudent, and that takes time.

It's important that you vet potential clients as quickly as possible. If they're flaky, don't waste your time proposing a scope of work for them because they're unlikely to hire you. How much should you vet your prospective clients? That's a gut call you'll need to make. But if you think a prospective client is flaky, then that's a red flag you'll want to pay attention to!

As part of a well-defined scope of work, you'll need to include what you intend to produce. There are a few other ways you can create rock-solid scopes of work to avoid the pitfalls that I didn't avoid in the past.

The first thing I often do is to list what is explicitly excluded from the scope of work. This is especially pertinent if the client, or a third party, must do something that will affect your work. In these cases, be sure to include in the written scope of work a statement that you will not be doing that thing.

Second, consider stating that only what's listed in the scope of work is included. You'd be surprised how many times I defined what I thought was a solid scope of work, but then, at the end of the project, the client thought I was going to do something else that wasn't listed. They had it in their mind that I'd do more even though we hadn't discussed it, and it wasn't in the scope of work. By the way, when you get into a situation like this, the client will try to get you to do that extra work without charging them! So always include a statement that effectively says that only what's listed is included.

Third, when the scope of work for a fixed price project changes, and it will, you must submit a change order. I would often explain to prospects that they can hire me by the hour or fixed price and that it's 100 percent their choice, really. I'd explain the pros and cons of each method.

I always recommended fixed price projects so they would have a budget for their project versus an unknown cost if they paid by the hour. But I caveated that with a fixed price project, we were setting up a system where I had to be relentless about tracking every requested change. If the scope changed and resulted in my having to do more work, but the price didn't change, that wouldn't work for me. It only works if the price changes when the scope changes.

That means you have to submit a change order for every change to the scope of work. And by every change, I mean every single change. You really should do this even for small changes that you won't charge for (submit a zero-dollar change order) to document that you are providing value without charging extra. Why go through the trouble of submitting a zero-dollar change order?

The client will always want changes. At the beginning of a project, you're likely to just make the changes to keep them happy. After all, you think you'll have plenty of chances to submit change orders later. Plus, you don't want to piss off your client in the beginning of the project, so you just do the extra work and don't charge them. Shoot, you may not even let them know that the change is taking you extra time. After all, you're a team player, right?

Here's the rub. At some point, after making a bunch of changes for free, you'll realize that it's time to start charging. The first time you bring up charging for a change, the client will ask you to throw it in at no cost. They'll say something like, "It's a small change, what's the big deal?"

And they'll be right. The problem is they forgot, or were never told, about all those other small changes that you did for free. Remember all those minor tweaks you made in the beginning of the project and didn't charge for? Actually, do you even remember all the changes you made for free? Since you didn't document those changes, then after the fact, you'll probably only have a foggy recollection of all the changes and the time it took to do each one. If you have a foggy recollection, trust me, your client doesn't remember at all or really didn't even realize it was a change to begin with.

So it's in your best interest to document every change made to the scope of work, even if you intend to do it for free. Start documenting these changes early in a project so that when the time comes to start charging for changes, you can remind your client of all the freebies you already threw in.

At a minimum, send them an email each time to say you did them a solid. That way, you can pull those up, remind them of the free value you previously provided, and justify why you now need to charge for the extra they're requesting.

Charging for change orders is a pain, but if you avoid this issue, it's at your own peril.

Although you have the opportunity to make more money with fixed price projects, you also have the ability to lose your ass. The amount of work that you may have to do, and at your cost, can far outweigh the benefit if you really screw things up.

Thankfully, that hasn't happened to me in any big way. In working on fixed price projects for several years, I never got myself into serious trouble, and I never lost money. I credit this to the basic attribute of paying attention and charging for change orders.

Generally speaking, I won more projects and made more money

because I was capable of working on fixed price projects. Moving from hourly billing to fixed price projects was a big deal for us. It resulted in us winning more projects, earning more profit per project, and allowing us to hire more people.

Fixed price projects were great.

That is, until I discovered an even better way of charging for work.

→ Recurring revenue

Although the change from working by the hour to fixed price projects was a big improvement, I had been hearing for a while about another model for pricing and getting paid—the recurring revenue model.

One of the problems I faced for years was that we'd work on a project with a client, do a fantastic job, hand over the work, and that was it. That was the end of us working with the client. There wasn't another opportunity to work with, or to make money from, the client that we just wowed. We were a "one and done" operation.

Certainly, we would request a testimonial and referrals, and of course we could add their project to our growing portfolio, but the opportunity to work with and monetize that client had passed. I wanted a way to continue working with the client, and getting paid by that client, after delivering the project. What other service could I offer to make that happen?

My first stab at solving that problem was to offer web hosting. Since the websites we built needed to run on servers, I thought, *Why not offer web hosting?* So we offered web hosting to a few clients, and they agreed to it.

We purchased a plan from a web hosting company and marked up the cost by 30 percent. Later I marked it up even more. Even though we were making a good percentage of profit on web hosting, it just wasn't that much money because web hosting is generally pretty cheap. Our hosting bill only cost about a hundred dollars a month, so we could only make about thirty dollars in profit. Big deal, right? With only a few of these clients, it amounted to peanuts. It certainly wasn't enough to pay many bills or help with payroll. Honestly, it was more trouble than it was worth to only make thirty dollars a month.

One afternoon I had lunch with the owner of a successful IT company. During lunch he explained how years earlier, he shifted away from a break/fix model to manage service. In the break/fix model, he'd only make money by fixing something that was broken—a computer, network, or similar piece of hardware. Basically, he was responding to a one-time emergency. Once he fixed the problem, his work with the client was over until the next time something broke.

With managed services, he and the client agreed upfront to a recurring set of services, many of them preventative, and a recurring price. The price was based on the number of people and computers the company had and that he would support. This led to more predictable work for him since those clients stayed even if something wasn't broken.

He also told me that he had been operating with 100 percent recurring revenue for the past few years, he loved it, and he would never go back to break/fix.

Walking back to my office after lunch, he asked me if we had recurring revenue. I told him about the pittance of hosting fees we collected. He encouraged me by saying that was good, but that I should try to figure out how to repackage what we already offered as a recurring service. He promised that if I could figure that out, then it would unlock all sorts of opportunities.

Back at the shop, I continued to think about it. Like every other web company on the planet, we sold websites to clients as projects. At the time, I hadn't yet figured out how to offer websites as a recurring service.

After delivering a website, clients always want changes. Some change requests come right after we deliver the new website, but many more come over time. These changes have to do with changes in their industry, market movements, pivots the company is making, updating content, new staff, and many other reasons. Almost without fail, every client will request changes over time.

Additionally, websites needed to be updated as internal and external software components are updated. Those are nerdy technical tasks, but they were important, nonetheless. As an example, we've found that the typical website needs two-and-a-half updates per week to stay current. Some of these updates include new features, and others are security patches. Fail to apply too many of these patches, and you're asking for your website to get hacked.

Knowing it's important to keep a website up today, and that clients will want changes over time, I decided to offer support packages as add-ons and after we delivered the new website. I also included intangibles such as us keeping the credentials to their systems so we could log in at a moment's notice if there was an issue. Keeping credentials didn't cost us anything, but I made an argument that we only kept credentials for clients because if we had them for non-clients, it was a liability. The argument, which I still make today, is that if someone happened to hack their applications, and we had the credentials in our possession, they could point to us as causing the problem.

I didn't want to hold that confidential information—credentials and access to their database—unless I was under contract to do so. Holding them was a liability, and I wanted to get paid for that liability so I could assure that we did it correctly. For clients, we'd safeguard those credentials, but we deleted credentials for past clients who declined our support packages. That meant they would be 100 percent on their own to manage their website.

I'd also ensure that someone on staff understood how to work on their system. This was a big intangible that cost real dollars.

After delivering a product, the person who built it could end up quitting the company. The potential for this happening increases as the application gets older. When that happens, you find yourself in a situation where no one understands how the website works. Yes, we can figure it out, but that takes between a few hours and several days.

If the person who built the website left the company, and no one else knew how to work on it, and then the client asked for a small change, it could turn into a big effort. The client wouldn't be happy if we charged, say, two hours for a small change that the previous developer could have done in ten minutes.

Without a support package, the client would be taking the risk that no one knew how to work on their site. With my support package, I took that risk, but for a fee, of course. I'd take the hit if I had to spin up a new developer on their website, and I'd essentially guarantee that someone would be able to make a quickie change whenever the client needed one.

I started successfully selling these plans at the end of most projects. Slowly, but surely, I was getting recurring revenue. But it still wasn't adding up to a lot of money.

Fast-forward to today. All of our revenue, 100 percent of our revenue, comes from recurring revenue. Once we switched to focusing on digital marketing, it was a natural fit. With digital marketing, clients continually need services such as social media posts, engagement with their audience, writing content for SEO purposes and newsletters, and creating, monitoring, and improving the effectiveness of online advertising campaigns.

Since we focus on helping companies with their marketing, we're with them for the long haul. We agree upfront to the services we'll provide on a recurring basis and how much that will cost every month. It's a win/win—clients know we're going to continually focus on their marketing, and we know they'll continue to be clients and pay us.

I even finally figured out how to charge for websites on a recurring basis. With the old model, which most of our competitors still cling to, there is one opportunity for them to monetize a new website. With that, they have to maximize the price regardless of the actual cost to build the website.

A marketing website typically costs $5,000 to $20,000, sometimes more. That's a lot to pay upfront. Once the new website is delivered, clients will want changes, which most agencies then charge $150/hour or more to make. If you use the agency for hosting, they charge for that separately, and if you need anything else, like new stock photos or a new security certificate, they'll charge you for that as well. Basically, you get nickeled and dimed as a client and have to buy everything à la carte. It starts to wear you out after a while.

Knowing I wanted recurring revenue and not project revenue, I beat my head against the wall until I figured it out. I eventually realized that I needed to stop thinking of the value of the website as a one-time transaction. After all, most of the websites we create don't take so much time to build that they even justify a $10,000-plus price tag.

I thought, *What if we essentially gave away a new website, but charged for all of the ongoing support and hosting fees?* What if we followed the model of the shaving-razor industry? Basically give away the handle and make our money on the razor blades instead? I wanted to wrap up all project and recurring work into a simple and consistent monthly fee.

If we did that, then we'd have to basically amortize the cost of the upfront work, as well as provide continuing value by making updates to clients' websites, patching them on a regular basis, hosting them, backing them up, and performing other background services to ensure they remained fast, healthy, and hack-free.

Once we broke our addiction to charging project fees for new websites, we had unlocked how we could offer everything we provide as a recurring service. We finally had our answer.

But Erik, what if you build the website and then the client leaves? You just created a brand-new website and only got paid for a month or two.

Correct. We had to be sure that the client would stick around for a while. For that reason, we require a minimum commitment of twelve months. If they stay longer, they'll still get all the same recurring services—changes, patches, backups—but we were guaranteed to get paid for at least a year.

But Erik, what if the client takes their website and leaves before a year is up?

Another great question. To ensure that a client can't just take their website elsewhere after a month or two, we always host their website on our server. We won't provide a backup to the website until after they've satisfied their minimum commitment of twelve months.

But Erik, what if they break the minimum commitment? Sure, you'll keep the website, but you won't get paid.

Valid point. This is a risk for sure, and it's happened before where clients simply default on their contract with us and stop paying the monthly fee. In that case, we don't hand over the website because they haven't finished paying for it. If you have a loan on a car and stop paying on it, it's not yours, and the repo man will come take it from you! Same with our websites. Although we have been screwed by this in the past, it's been few and far between.

Having addressed all those concerns, and after having priced websites as a service for a couple of years now, it turns out this model works. Actually, it works incredibly well. Clients love that they don't have to stroke a big check upfront and then get nickeled and dimed later for ongoing services. They love that they have a long-term partner they can call on for whatever change they want, and we'll get it done at no extra fee.

In turn, we love the recurring revenue that websites bring. Sure, it takes our web designers a week or more of concentrated effort to create a new website, but after that we continue to get paid month after month. We've aligned our interests with our clients' interests, on websites and all of our services, and it's a winner.

Recurring revenue brought forth a number of other improvements to the business that I didn't expect at first. Once we began getting most of our revenue from recurring services, we realized that we still had business practices in place that just weren't necessary.

One example is timesheets. When we worked by the hour, we had to have our staff meticulously report how much time they worked on each project, what they did, and for how long. This was a daily chore put on everyone in the company.

Invoices to our clients derived from those timesheets, so I wanted to make sure that timesheet entries were accurate. Tracking all that data is time-consuming and meticulous. It's easy to make mistakes. That meant that someone had to review all timesheet entries before invoices were generated to ensure clients got accurate invoices. Guess who got that task? Yep, me.

The whole time-tracking process was a huge pain for those tracking time, and for me who had to spend hours reviewing timesheet entries. It seemed like we were fighting a losing battle trying to get everyone to fill in these stupid timesheets, and it was getting worse as the company grew.

We carried the practice of time-tracking forward even after we switched to recurring revenue.

We continued to track time simply because that's the way we thought companies operated. We had always tracked time and, like it or not, that's just what agencies do. After all, other agencies we looked up to did it, so it must be smart, right?

Wrong.

After much debate and thinking through the impact of the change, we stopped collecting time. We simply stopped caring about how much time went into a project. No longer wanting to track time, we canceled the subscription to our time-tracking software. No longer burdened with the daily chore of filling out timesheets for every project, everyone was happier.

Another great thing about recurring revenue is that your finances are predictable. Our original CPA once asked Kevin and me how the next quarter was shaping up for us. At the time, we were doing project work almost exclusively. My response to the CPA was something along the lines of, "I don't know ... we could double our revenue next month or we could go out of business."

That's the problem with revenue that's not recurring. There's a saying in entrepreneurship that you eat what you kill. With project work, you don't even know what's available to be killed until it walks up to you.

Although we were getting pretty lucky that clients with projects kept coming to us, we simply had no way of predicting how many projects would come our way in the future. Any prediction was a wild guess. I hated that feeling.

With recurring revenue, we're not only able to project our finances out next month, but for as long as we'd like. Since our clients pay us the same amount month after month, the only thing that will change is if we get more clients, which I'm glad to report happens on a regular basis, or if a client drops us. As long as we monitor if our clients are happy with us, which we do, we anticipate problems before they happen. The goal with recurring revenue is to preserve what you have and get more of it.

Since our revenue and the services we provide are consistent, so are our expenses. With recurring revenue, I finally have the ability to see into the future and confidently predict where we'll be next quarter, next year, and beyond.

The benefits of recurring revenue go on and on. I could write another book focused exclusively on recurring revenue. Like the IT company owner who encouraged me, I highly encourage you to find a way to obtain recurring revenue. Look at your project pricing practices and focus on ways you could transform them into recurring services.

Let's say my limo buddy, whom I mentioned before, wants to transition to recurring revenue. Instead of charging clients each time they use the limo, imagine if he offered them a subscription. If his best customers pay $500 each time they use the limo, but only use it two to three times a year, what if he instead offered them a subscription of $150 per month to use it up to three times a year?

Instead of collecting between $1,000 and $1,500 a year, he could collect $150 every month. If he did that, he'd guarantee to earn $1,800 a year on the customer instead of just $500 each time the customer called. As a perk, he could offer a VIP service for these kinds of customers. Perks like priority booking over non-VIP customers and a bottle of champagne in the limo every time. Those perks may not cost the company that much more, but his customers will be wowed by his customer service.

Another example of where recurring services could work well is with clothing. My tailor runs a shop where he has suits, shoes, and high-end casual wear for sale. Each time I go in to get something tailored, I look at his displays, and I usually buy an item that costs around $200. It's great to come home with a new piece of high-quality clothing, but I only buy from him when I need something tailored and go to his shop, which is about once a year.

Instead of selling only by the item, and only selling to me once a year, what if he created a VIP club? Let's say I paid him a hundred dollars a month to be in the club. As a VIP, he could send me a newsletter letting me know what's in fashion and what he recommends for me. He could track my wardrobe and make recommendations based on what he knows I already own. Every month I'd pay the $100 whether I got something or not.

When I needed something, or when his marketing convinced me that I needed something, I could use whatever funds had accumulated to pay for it. So one month I may buy only a tie, but two months later I may buy an expensive sports coat. If he created a VIP club, then it would help me keep my wardrobe up to date, which I surely would appreciate, and it would keep revenue coming in the door for him in between my visits to get something tailored.

Every business is different. Think about what you sell to your customers as a project, and rethink about how you could sell it to them as a recurring service. Once you unlock that, and once you unlock recurring revenue, you've created a predictable business for yourself.

→ Payment terms

"Payment terms" refers to how long a client has before paying your invoice. From my early Navy contracting days, I had learned that Net 30 was the norm. At least in that business, it was.

The "Net" in Net 30 means that the person or company being invoiced has thirty days from the date of the invoice to pay it in full. Net also refers to the balance due after all discounts are applied. So let's say I give you an invoice on December 1 for $1,000, apply a $50 discount, and payment terms are Net 30. You'd be expected to pay $950 no later than December 31.

Many clients will request payment terms from you. The rationale is that once they receive your invoice, they need time to review it, approve it, and send you the payment. The larger the company, the longer it will take you to get paid.

The longest payment terms, also simply referred to as "terms," that I've ever agreed to was Net 45. That happened when I was still a young company, wanted to work for a somewhat large regional corporation, and frankly, I needed the work. Although I agreed to Net 45, it was confusing because most of my clients were on Net 30 and this one was different. That meant we had an administrative burden of keeping track of what payment terms we had extended to which client. It's important to know the terms given to each client so you know when each client's invoice is late.

I've heard other entrepreneurs talk about clients who demand Net 45, Net 60, and even longer. The longer you go without getting paid, the more susceptible you are to cash flow crunches.

Earlier I used the example of submitting an invoice on December 1 with Net 30 terms and the due date of December 31. But here's how it would likely play out ...

Let's say you're working on a long-term project by the hour. Terms are Net 30, and you can only invoice once a month, which is also pretty standard. That means you start working on November 1 and work all month through November 30. On December 1, you can run a report that shows how many hours were worked for the client during the previous month, multiply by the billable rate, and send the invoice that day.

If you're efficient, then you, your admin, or your accountant will send out the invoice on December 1. But more likely than not, there will be questions about individual time charges. Remember when I said it would take me hours to review time charges submitted by my team? It would also take days for them to turn in all of their hours before I could even do my review. All those delays add up.

What if I had a busy day on December 1 and couldn't get to it that day? The invoice will be delayed. What if I couldn't get to it the next day? Another delay. Once I finally got to it, I needed clarification from someone on the team, but they were on vacation. Another delay. And what if the clock didn't start ticking on December 1 because that was a Saturday, and we waited until Monday, December 3, to start this process ... another delay. Unless you're on top of time charges on a regular basis, as in every day you're reviewing charges as they happen, the invoice generated in December for the work performed in November will be delayed due to your own administrative overhead.

You finally get the invoice out a few days into December, let's say December 6. The day that you create the invoice is technically when the clock starts ticking for the client, even if they haven't received the invoice yet. But practically, if there's a delay in them receiving it, then you'll often adjust your invoice date out of fairness to them.

It's in your best interest to get the invoice to your client as soon as it's produced. Any delay between when you produce it and when they receive it can result in a delay in your payment being processed and a delay in you getting your money.

For that reason, we email all of our invoices to clients. We also email because printing an invoice, stuffing the invoice into an envelope, stamping the envelope, and getting the envelope to the post office will incur labor and time on our side. There's also the expense of paper and postage, and this whole process will delay the invoice going out.

Mind you, you paid your people, you paid rent, and you incurred all other expenses throughout November when you were doing the work. In early December, as you work to create the invoice, you also have the administrative expense of creating the invoice. Then as you wait for the payment to arrive, you're continuing to pay those same expenses.

The client receives your invoice for work performed in November on, say, December 6. They'll know that the earliest they have to pay is January 6. Even though they may be able to pay you sooner, they are unlikely to do so because they'd prefer to keep the cash in their bank account. After all, you're not even expecting payment until January 6, so why would they pay you sooner?

Sometimes a client won't mail you the check until the due date. In that case, if the mail goes out on January 6, you won't get it until the 9th or 10th. Other times, clients will intentionally pay a little late. They may delay payment a few days or a week. No big deal, right? But that just pushed payment out for you until around January 15 or so. You may not receive payment until mid-January or later for work you started paying for in November!

Since you're doing the work for a client, and they're going to pay you later, you've effectively extended them credit. You've given them a line of credit, and you're spending your own money on their project while hoping they will pay you back. Even though you've given them credit, chances are you didn't have them fill out a credit application and probably have no idea how likely they are to even be able to pay you back.

Isn't this a crazy system? Working on credit means that you're at risk of not getting paid. The smaller and the newer the client, the more risk that you won't get paid. In the past ten years, I've had multiple clients stiff me. I funded their operations without so much as running a credit check on them, and then they never paid me.

But Erik, if they don't pay you, can't you just sue them?

One client who stiffed me had been paying all along until we delivered the final product. A few days later, we delivered the last invoice. He said he'd pay that last invoice, but days turned into weeks, which turned into months, and the payment never showed up. I finally had my lawyers take action on him and we won a judgment for the full amount. But even a judgment against someone will not ensure you'll get paid.

With the judgment in hand, my lawyers said we could submit a garnishment order to his bank to collect from his account balance. All they needed was a copy of a previous check he gave me, and they'd submit the judgment to his bank and his bank would be forced to pay us. How cool is that?

I dug up copies of the checks that the client had used to pay us, and gave them to our lawyers. They submitted the garnishment forms to the bank. A few days later, the bank responded, rejecting our garnishment request. Turned out that our contract and judgment were for an LLC that the client formed for the project, but the check he used to pay us was from his other business. The two didn't match.

The garnishment paperwork was for a different company than the company that controlled the bank account he had been paying us from. That was the end of the line for pursuing collecting a few thousand from that client.

Although I didn't get paid for the work we did, it was a huge lesson learned for me. It emphasized that offering payment terms is literally extending credit to clients. The credit worthiness of your client needs to be taken into consideration.

With that, I had my lawyers draft a personal guarantee. On a case-by-case basis, I had clients sign the personal guarantee for the next year or so. With a personal guarantee, the person signing the contract commits the company, and themselves personally, to paying us.

But I stopped using personal guarantees shortly thereafter because I learned a more valuable lesson: Don't work with untrustworthy clients.

Also, get paid upfront.

When you get paid in advance, it doesn't matter as much if they one day stop paying you. Sure, you lose out on anticipated revenue, but at least you'll have minimized the work you do for free.

To summarize payment terms, it's in your best interest to make them as short as possible. Net 30 is better than Net 90, but Net 15 is better than Net 30.

Always try to shorten the amount of time it takes for you to get paid. The longer the terms, the longer you're funding your client's project, and the more at risk you are for nonpayment.

→ **Lines of credit**

The longer you wait to get paid, the more likely it is that you'll run low on money. In extreme cases, you could run out of money waiting to get paid. In business, running out of money is a bad thing! Avoid it at all costs.

This is when a line of credit loan (LOC) comes in handy.

With an LOC, you get preapproved to borrow up to a certain amount of money, but you can borrow in smaller amounts as needed. LOCs get you through the low points in times of cash flow crunches when you're waiting to get paid.

Let's say that while you're waiting to receive a big payment on an invoice, your bank account balance dips low. So low that it either makes you nervous or you're unable to pay other bills or payroll. You can borrow money from your LOC to get you through the cash crunch while you wait for your invoice to get paid. Once you get paid, you can pay the LOC back in part or in full.

When's the best time to open an LOC? Any time before you actually need it. Like any other loan, it takes time to process your loan request. You must fill out paperwork, get approved, and sign documents. All that can take weeks.

When you submit the paperwork, your bank will want to see your finances for the previous and current years. If they see that you're not doing very well, they may not approve your loan request. Or they may approve you for an amount lower than you requested.

If you're not in need of an LOC now, then now is the perfect time to submit for it because your finances are probably looking pretty good. Apply for the loan, get as large of an LOC as they'll give you, and it'll be in place when times get tough. Get it now while you can, and let it sit there until you need it.

→ Getting paid upfront

In a perfect world, you'd get paid in advance of starting the work. That way the money is in the bank and the client funds their work versus you having to scrape your money together to fund it.

Imagine if you got paid Net -30, as in thirty days before you even started the work. The money would just be sitting there and you should rarely, if ever, have to worry about cash flow. Getting paid way in advance is cash flow utopia. It happens sometimes, but is rare.

A much more realistic scenario is Net 0, which is what we now aim for at Array Digital. What I mean by that is that we get paid the same day we invoice, and the same day we start for the next month. Actually, we don't invoice the client, we send them a sales receipt because they pay when billed. Here's how we pull that off.

When we onboard a new client, we stress to them that we accept ACH—Automated Clearing House—payments. ACH means that we have the ability, and permission, to withdraw our payment directly from our clients' bank accounts. So on the day of the month that we charge a client, we process an ACH payment and get funded immediately.

Since we focus exclusively on recurring revenue, we always bill the client the same amount on the same day of the month. It's highly predictable, all-inclusive pricing, and spelled out in our contracts. With that, there's no need for our clients to require extra time to review and process an invoice. Net terms are no longer needed.

We also accept credit card payments. Credit card payments aren't as good for us because we incur a credit card fee, typically 3 percent of the total charged. But I'd rather pay that and be 99 percent sure I'll get paid on Net 0 than have to wait for a check to arrive and clear before getting paid. But there's another downside to accepting credit cards—chargebacks.

A client could dispute your credit card charge after it's been approved and after you've been paid. When that happens, the credit card company immediately withdraws the disputed amount from your bank account and then notifies you of the chargeback. They take the money back before you even have a chance to plead your case.

There's technically an appeals process that allows you to explain why you should get paid. But in my experience, I've never won one of these appeals, and I've appealed at least a dozen throughout the years.

Credit card companies always seem to side with the customer. Because of the possibility of chargebacks and the hefty fees, we discourage payments by credit cards.

We still have clients who pay by check. I prefer to not have clients pay by check, but some insist, and if we don't allow it, then it could be a deal breaker. In the end, I'm willing to take a little risk every once in a while on payment terms. But I make sure to cap our risk.

When a client has decided not to pay by ACH or credit card, and insists on paying by check, then we strictly enforce payment terms and late fees. They get a warning on the due date if their invoice isn't paid in full, and seven days later we hit them with late fees.

After completing a few projects for my first Elance client, she realized the legacy technology she initially had me working on was so inefficient and outdated that she needed it replaced. I gave her a fixed price quote of $18,000. She accepted but asked if it was okay if she extended the payments to as long as she needed to eventually pay me off. Eager to get the work, and very naive, I agreed.

As I started to work on the project, she requested changes. Each change resulted in a change order that she agreed to. She made small payments of about $500 a month even as the amount owed continued to increase. She requested more changes, which I made. The balance due continued to climb until one day I realized she had accumulated a balance of $35,000!

I was shocked when I realized how much she owed. Especially so when the payments slowed down substantially. I realized I was in a pickle. She lived in a different state than me, and I had never met her in person. I knew little about her and didn't have a solid contract vetted by a lawyer at the time.

Think I had her fill out a credit app first? Nope, of course not. Who does that? Jeez, what was I thinking? I was really exposed and at risk for getting stiffed. All I had was her word that she would pay me.

I also realized that since I wasn't charging her late fees, and other creditors like credit card companies were, it was in her best interest to pay off the other creditors before me. I had allowed her to get seriously in debt with me, and I had volunteered to go to the back of the line for those waiting to get paid. That is not a good place to be.

She eventually made good and paid me 100 percent, but it took about two years. What a relief when that final payment was made! I learned a valuable lesson. Never wanting to be at the back of the line again, I decided I had to start charging late fees.

I hate the process of trying to collect payment for work I've already done. It's a huge waste of time and money to create a collection process. I didn't go into business to become a collection agency, and I no longer mess around with that.

The payment terms we now offer ensure we get paid at the beginning of each month. Worst case, a check doesn't come in for a couple of weeks and we'll suspend a client for nonpayment. At least we'll only lose payment for a few weeks of services, not months. I'd much rather just get paid by ACH or credit card and be done with it.

When it comes to payment terms, don't automatically give in to long terms. Always try to get better terms. You deserve to get paid, and paid quickly. Any delay in getting paid puts you at risk. If you take too much risk and it doesn't work out in your favor, you'll run out of money. When you run out of money, the game is over.

As the founder and operator of your company, making sure you don't run out of money is one of your main responsibilities. A significant one at that. You cannot run out of money. The longer payment terms you offer, the higher the chances that you'll have cash flow issues and potentially run out of money.

→ Paying yourself

One of the hardest parts of becoming an entrepreneur is the unpredictability of your finances. With a day job you get a predictable paycheck. Not so with running your own business.

> Most people are familiar with the formula:
> Revenue − Expenses = Profit.

Guess what part of the formula your pay comes from? You pay yourself from profit—what's left over after you pay all of your company expenses. But not all of your profits will go toward your pay because profit is needed elsewhere in the company too.

Your business needs to accumulate a financial cushion in the bank for surprises and to withstand cash flow crunches, like when your clients don't pay on time or for economic downturns. You'll also want to reinvest some of your profits back into your company so you can grow. In reality, only about one-third to one-half of your profits should go toward your pay.

The amount that you need to pay yourself is directly linked to your lifestyle. To determine the right pay for yourself, evaluate how much profit your company is making and how much you need to live. You may need to reconcile the two if your company isn't making quite enough to fund your lifestyle.

Your lifestyle is comprised of three different types of expenses:

1. The expenses you must pay
2. The expenses you want to pay
3. Bullshit wasteful spending

We're going to approach these in reverse order starting with the third bullet: bullshit wasteful spending.

Bullshit wasteful spending refers to expenses you can easily do without. I'm talking about going out, buying rounds of drinks at a bar, eating out at restaurants, splurging on entertainment, buying new clothes, and subscribing to multiple music and media accounts. When you first start off on your own, all that needs to go bye-bye.

But Erik...

Nope, sorry. There's just no excuse for wasting your money when you first step out on your own. Cut it out immediately.

Besides, you need to be totally obsessed with your business if you want it to succeed. There will be little downtime to go out anyway. You won't need new clothes—wear your old ones. Do with what you have and save your money as you work to get your business off the ground.

The second category of expenses are those that you want to pay for. I'm talking about your nice car, your gym membership, a new phone, even where you live. All of these things can likely be downgraded. If you want.

Do you really need a new BMW with a $700/month payment, or will an eight-year-old car with a $155/month payment suffice for now? Do you really need to live in that dope condo downtown for $1,750/month, or is it worth it to move in with a friend, split the rent, and reduce your rent to $750/month?

It comes down to personal choice. It also comes down to whether you can afford it. I'm not saying you have to cut these things, but you should acknowledge that they can be cut if needed.

Everyone will have a different level they're willing to cut down to, and everyone also has different stakeholders (e.g., spouse, children) who get a vote on this too. Think about what you could cut if needed, and at least put a rough plan together. If times get tough, cut a bit more into this second category of spending.

The last category we'll touch on are expenses you must pay. Those are things like food, utilities, internet, and housing—your basic requirements. You can cut some luxury out of the "expenses you want to pay," but you need a roof over your head and can't cut out but so much of these required expenses. You can't do much about these kinds of expenses. This is what I refer to as your base level of living expenses.

When I went off on my own, I had a conversation with my wife about finances. We had to cut the bullshit expenses. Luckily, I already had some clients and we were bringing in revenue. I didn't have a lot of luxury items, and I could continue to pay for the expenses that I wanted and needed like my house and my car. Really, I didn't need to cut much at all. I had saved up a nice financial buffer, and I had a service that people needed.

That last part was the key for me, so I'll repeat it. I had a service that was in demand. That's so important and is why I recommend that new entrepreneurs validate their idea before doing anything else. Will someone buy what you're selling?

Pay yourself from your profits, and fund the gap between what your company can pay you and what you need with the money you saved from your day job and from your freelancing.

Once you've looked at your personal living expenses and cut out the bullshit, how are you going to pay yourself? There are two ways to do this. The most common way is to take whatever is left over from profits as you need to pay personal bills. That means that as your personal bills come due—e.g., car payment, house payment—you take money out of the company and pay for those personal bills. I've done this in the past, and what it amounts to is erratically paying yourself. I also felt tremendously guilty each time I took money out of the bank and worried that I was being too greedy at the expense of my business.

Your company needs money. Sometimes badly. And paying yourself only what's left over means that you constantly subjugate your personal needs to the needs of the business. If you're single and are okay with a monk-life lifestyle while you build up your company, then this kind of life may be just fine for you. Take from the company only when you need to. But if you're married with kids, or in a similar situation, you and your family probably need a bit more.

After paying myself erratically for a solid year and fretting about it every time I took money out of the company for myself, and after many "intense discussions" about finances with my wife, I switched to the second way of paying oneself. The opposite of erratically paying yourself is to set it and forget it.

I set my salary and paid myself on a consistent basis. The salary that I selected was enough to pay my bills—house, car, food, gas—and just a bit more. But I wasn't funding an extravagant lifestyle.

I set myself up on salary and I always paid myself the same amount on the same frequency. This was technically accomplished with a scheduled transfer from my business bank account to my personal bank account. That provided me with stability in my personal finances. And on the company side, I knew what I needed to set aside for my most valuable employee—me!

In addition to the base salary, I paid myself a portion of profits—about one-third. I'd look back at the previous month, calculate profits, and cut myself a check. Sometimes that was a small amount, sometimes it was bigger, and sometimes it didn't happen at all.

As time went on, my business matured, and as the finances became more predictable, this "bonus" also became more predictable.

I've never been one to pull too much out of the company for myself. I'd prefer to live a modest to slightly-above-modest lifestyle and keep the funds in the company to fuel its growth. It will take a long time for me to grow the company to where I want it to go, and the company will require a lot of cash. I have to build up my personal nest egg, but I have to build up the company first before I extract riches. That time will come. But for the foreseeable future, we're in a building mode.

So now it's time for you to figure out how to pay yourself. I would start by paying yourself only what you need to survive. Then as time goes on, and if your company is making more money and profit, increase the amount you take out to help your personal finances even more. Then when your company can support it, determine a set amount to withdraw on a regular basis and automate your pay.

Chapter takeaways

1. Billing by the hour is the easiest way to start charging clients, but it's also limiting. You can only make more money if you put in more time.
2. With fixed price projects, you have the opportunity to charge more based on the value of the work you are doing. Fixed price projects allow you to separate how much time you put into a project from the amount you charge.
3. Both billing by the hour and fixed price projects don't provide a lot of predictability into your future finances.

4. Recurring revenue is the most sought-after type of revenue.
5. With recurring revenue, you can accurately predict your future revenue and expenses and start to determine your growth trajectory.
6. Test creative ways that you can switch from billing by the hour, or by the project, to a recurring revenue model.
7. Minimize your payment terms. You always want to be paid sooner rather than later for the work you do for your clients.
8. Lines of credit can help with cash flow problems.
9. The best time to get a line of credit from a bank is when you don't need one. When you apply, get as large of a line of credit as you can. You may need it later.
10. Always try to get paid upfront. You can accomplish this by charging when your invoices, or sales receipts, are sent. Set your terms and expectations early on with clients, and collect your money via ACH.
11. When starting out, pay yourself the minimum needed to pay for your must-have personal expenses, like a car and home. Cut out the unnecessary expenses, like dining out.
12. As time goes on and your company makes more profit, begin to settle into a set amount you'll pay yourself from the company on a predetermined basis.

→ 09

Managing the money

One of your most significant responsibilities as a founder is to ensure that you get your finances straight. Overspend and run out of money, and you're done.

Sure, some companies borrow from venture capitalists and overspend like it's going out of style. For everyone else who is building something from the ground up and doesn't want to chase a pipe dream and answer to a board of directors, just remember ... don't run out of money!

→ Raising capital

Many potential entrepreneurs cite a lack of funds as the reason they haven't started their own business. They believe they have to raise money, yet they have no clue how to go about finding funding. Worse, they don't even know why they think they need funding.

I'm just not a fan of raising funds. When I ask these "wantrepreneurs" if it's possible to fund their business from their operational profits, they either agree that it's possible or come up with an excuse.

I've launched more businesses than I care to admit, and I have never borrowed money. It's not because I inherited a trust fund or because I'm rich. Instead I've invested the minimum amount of my own money needed to start the company, then I validated the idea by having someone buy what I was selling.

With my first few businesses, I made the mistake of waiting too long to validate my idea. I built everything to perfection (confession ... I wanted perfection but rarely achieved it), which took way too much time and money. Once built, then I tried to sell it.

But after learning the hard way by wasting time and money, I realized that the sooner you validate your idea, the better. As quickly and inexpensively as possible, build an offering with minimum core functionality, without all the bells and whistles, and then try to get someone to buy it. This approach is referred to as the Minimal Viable Product (MVP).

If you have success in selling the first version of your offering, then invest a bit more time and money into a better version. Then sell that version to another customer. Continue to ratchet your way toward a better, more legitimate offering one step at a time, selling all along the way.

This approach works extremely well with a service offering that doesn't require a significant capital investment. Since you don't have to buy much, if anything, before you start offering your service, you can generally get into business quickly. No external funding is required.

Well Erik ... I need a truck and tools! I need funding.

Do you though? Do you really need to start with a brand-new $50,000 truck and a whole assortment of brand-new, top-end tools? Or could you start with your current vehicle and the tools you already own? Do that, start simply, make money, and reinvest that money back into better tools. Continue to sell and service, and continue to reinvest in your business.

Eventually you'll have the down payment on that new truck and will be making enough to cover the payments. Little by little ... see how that works? You don't have to start with everything perfect on day one.

I've never raised money, so I don't know what it's like. But I'm aware that it's a huge distraction away from running your business. Instead of focusing on your offering, your customers, or your delivery, entrepreneurs focus on chasing funding from angels and venture capitalists. They focus on their pitch deck and traveling around to pitch it to potential investors. The process of pitching is completely different than running your business. It will be stressful, a time sink, and that'll be your priority instead of building your business.

If that weren't bad enough, if you're successful in raising capital, then you've just worked your way into a job. Congratulations, you now have a boss! The investors who gave you money will likely have a significant equity stake in the company, and thus, a significant say and influence in how you "do your own thing."

But worse, they'll have high demands of you. They'll make demands that they believe will help you to pay them back. They will give you direction as to how to run your company, who to hire, who to fire, what markets to enter into or exit from, and on what timelines. They'll be all over you if they don't agree with your approach. Shoot, they could even fire you from the company you started!

Is that what you want? I doubt it.

It may work out amazingly for others, but that's not the life I want, and I doubt you want that either.

Don't get me wrong ... if I could be the founder of the next Facebook, then yah, it'd be worth it. But my business ideas aren't exactly shattering the paradigm for how we interact as a species. I get that some big, high-risk businesses necessitate raising funds. My business ideas are much more practical and less capital intensive, and I don't want to give away equity and control to grow the business even faster than it's growing on its own.

My advice on raising capital: skip it and focus on your business, not on borrowing money.

→ **Taxes**

I'm sure you've heard Benjamin Franklin's popular saying, "There are only two things certain in life: death and taxes."

Like it or not, you will pay taxes once you start your own company. Paying taxes on the money you earn is not a new concept. You pay taxes at your day job too, but your employer made it easy by taking your taxes out of your paycheck before you got the rest. They take care of that messiness for you.

Not so as an entrepreneur. You will be subject to taxation and in many different ways.

Some taxes you can't do anything about, such as your business license. It's actually a tax, but it's rarely referred to as a tax. It certainly sounds better to call it a license than a straight-up tax, which it is. A business license tax is calculated from the gross revenue of your company. There's nothing you can do to change the amount you'll get taxed besides lying about your revenue. By the way, don't do that. If you get audited and get caught, you'll face big fines and maybe even criminal charges. You're just going to have to suck it up, tell the government your revenue, and pay the tax bill.

Other taxes will be calculated on your profit. As a business, you are not taxed by the state or federal government on revenue. You are taxed on the profits. As a simplistic example, if your annual revenue is $100,000 and your expenses are $80,000, then you'll be taxed on the $20,000 profit.

The higher your profit, the more taxes you'll pay. Conversely, if your profit is low, then you'll pay a low amount of taxes. That can actually be a good thing. How is making less profit a good thing?

Let's say that you make a profit of $10,000, subject to tax at, say, 30 percent. That means you'll pay $3,000 to the state and feds, and keep $7,000. With that $7,000, you can pay yourself, put it in the bank, reinvest it in your business, or some combination of the three.

Instead of recognizing a $10K profit, let's say that you instead increase your expenses and put some of that $10K in profit back to work in your business immediately. You would do this by buying something you need, such as a piece of equipment or a laptop, or by hiring someone. You could even use the full $10K in your business to grow your business. In this scenario, you had $10K to put toward the advancement of your business. In the first scenario, you had only $7K to do the same.

Some entrepreneurs aim to operate at a low profit or no profit at all. They'll avoid paying substantial taxes, and they'll have additional funds to put into their business. By having little left over in the way of profits, you pay less in taxes and have more to put back into your company to grow it. It's a strategy for growth but also comes at the expense of not accumulating cash, which you may need for cash flow crunches or to weather a recession.

If you leverage this strategy, be sure to spend your profits on expenses that will move you forward. Don't spend wastefully—only buy what you need or think you'll need to advance your business.

As an entrepreneur, your pay is largely tied to your company profits, and often those profits are hard to predict. Since you no longer have an employer that withholds taxes from your pay, you're going to have to do that yourself. On a quarterly basis, the state and federal government want you to file Quarterly Estimated Taxes. So once a quarter, every three months, you should look back at the profit you earned for the previous quarter and calculate the taxes you owe as a result.

The tax forms have formulas for how to calculate the taxes you owe. You can do it yourself, but honestly, it's a royal pain. I swore off doing my own taxes many years ago. I simply don't want to invest my limited brain power into understanding the archaic tax code, and I don't want the financial liability of miscalculating my tax bill. I have a CPA for that.

I encourage you to do the same because I can't tell you how to calculate your tax bill. If you want to do that on your own, Godspeed to you. Instead I encourage you to put that energy into your business and let the CPAs do what they do best.

Although I defer the actual tax calculation to my CPA, I don't defer how much to set aside for the bill. I know I have to pay taxes, and I know roughly how much money I'll need based on my revenue and profit. I don't want to be surprised by a tax bill, or worse, not have the money set aside when it's due. So I put money aside on a regular basis, and I recommend you do the same in your business.

→ Business bank accounts

When I opened my freelancing business, I also opened a business checking account at the same bank that I use for my personal banking. With that, I had a second login, and the bank treated me as two separate entities: Erik the individual and Erik the person who ran a business. Two separate entities, two logins, two separate bank accounts.

When I made money from the business, it first went into the business account. Later when I was ready to pay myself, which felt great by the way, I would transfer money from the business account to my personal account. Since I used the same bank for my personal and business banking, it was an easy and instantaneous transfer. Money regularly flowed from my business to my personal accounts, but didn't flow from my personal to the business accounts.

There are only a few times that money should flow from your personal bank account to your business account. When you first open your business account, you'll likely want to put personal money in there. That simply jumpstarts the cash flow your business will need to get going.

Later, if your business is ever short on cash, then you may need to again move some funds from your personal account into your business account. It's not ideal, and hopefully these exceptions will be rare. If it happens more than occasionally, you should consider it as your business screaming at you that something is wrong. Your business should be making you money, not costing you money!

I had to fund my company on a few occasions in the past, but it didn't happen often. This happened early in my freelancing career, when I wasn't exactly overwhelmed with client work and flush with cash. It worked out in the end but was stressful at the time.

As time progressed, I opened accounts at different banks. It's wise to keep your profits and money needed to pay taxes in a different bank. This will intentionally make it harder for you to get your hands on the money. You should not use profits or tax money as a loan to pay for operating expenses, and keeping that money in another bank keeps the money out of sight and out of mind. We did exactly that and opened accounts at another bank.

Yes, it's a lot to have a dozen or more bank accounts across two to three banks. But honestly, it's not that confusing because each bank we use, and each bank account we have, serves a different purpose. One bank is for daily operating funds with bank accounts for each funding need (e.g., funds deposited, employee taxes, petty cash, general operating expenses). Our second bank is for securing profits and funds needed to pay quarterly taxes (in two separate bank accounts). And we now have a third bank that we stood up in order to fund new business ventures.

Sure, it makes the bookkeeping a bit more complicated because there are more accounts to track and more statements to reconcile. But it's a model that works well for me because I can look at the balance of any of these accounts and quickly determine how we're doing.

Do yourself a favor when you start making money. Separate your business money from your personal money by opening a business banking account. Eventually, you can open multiple accounts at multiple banks, like I did. But first things first—separate your cash between business and personal.

→ Profit First

I read an amazing book about business finances named Profit First by Mike Michalowicz. He lays out a system that allows you to easily set aside money for profits, taxes, salary, and other known expenses. We've been following the process religiously since I read the book a few years ago.

It's worked so well that I feel compelled to explain it here. It's so important to running a successful business that not including it would be a disservice to you. But this is just an overview. Buy his book, read it cover to cover, and then implement it. You can thank me later.

In the previous section on paying yourself, I shared the common formula: Revenue – Expenses = Profit. The Profit First philosophy reorganizes the formula to:

Revenue – Profit = Expense

Here's the big idea in a nutshell—pay yourself first. You've heard that saying when it comes to personal savings, but most entrepreneurs don't apply it to their business finances, for some reason. The book rationalizes creating a system so that you pay yourself a percentage of revenue for salary, taxes, and profit, and then your business expenses need to fit into whatever money is left over. Profits first, then expenses.

The system prescribed in the book includes depositing new revenue into a checking account dedicated just for this purpose. We'll call that account INCOME. As you get paid, you deposit the funds into INCOME and simply let it build up.

Twice a month, you'll transfer funds from the INCOME account to other bank accounts that serve specific purposes such as EMPLOYEE TAXES, OWNER TAXES, PROFIT, and OPEX (aka Operating Expenses). The amount you put into each is based on a predefined percentage of your annual revenue, which he helps you establish.

Let's say that you accumulate $10,000 in the INCOME account after two weeks. When it's time to disburse funds to the other accounts, all $10,000 will be sent to the other accounts. If you're putting aside, say, 10 percent for owner taxes, then $1,000 goes to the OWNER TAXES bank account and the rest goes to the other bank accounts based on your percentages.

So $1,000 is now in your OWNER TAXES bank account, just sitting there waiting to be paid to the government one day. It's best to no longer consider that your money. It's the government's money. Don't mess with it. Don't be tempted to "borrow" against it.

When it's time to pay quarterly taxes, and when your CPA tells you how much to pay to the state and to the feds, write checks out of your OWNER TAXES bank account. Although I hate to see the money go away, having it set aside in a special bank account dedicated to paying taxes takes the sting out of making the payment.

Having the money set aside brings me great relief. Before starting with the Profit First model, we would make tax payments out of our single Operating Expenses checking account. That's where all our money went in and all our money went out. It was always scary to write a big check out of there because I was never confident I knew how much money I would need for payroll, rent, and even my pay.

You're probably shaking your head at me ... *You didn't know how much money you needed, Erik?*

Nope.

The truth is that I always focused on running and growing the business. As long as there's money in the bank, I'm good, right? That's how most entrepreneurs think. If there's more money in the bank than expected, we'd loosen up and maybe spend a bit more. But if there was less in the bank than expected, we'd tighten up and spend less. We'd check our balances and make gut decisions. That's how we operated, and my guess is that you're pretty similar.

Profit First acknowledges our natural tendencies to make business decisions based on the balance of our bank account. What's great about Profit First is that it doesn't try to change our human nature. It just shifts the known expenses into different buckets for us so that we can set aside that money for intended purposes. It's a great system to help you manage money in a fast and easy way that doesn't fight your natural inclinations.

→ Expenses

As prescribed by Profit First, we have many different bank accounts, each with a specific purpose.

One of the accounts is called OPEX, short for Operating Expenses. It's used for everything except our owners' salary, taxes, and company profits. For us, our biggest expense is payroll. Beyond that, we have a slew of bills.

I've already mentioned that you need an accountant or a CPA. I currently have a payroll company that processes employee payroll and payroll taxes, a CPA who helps us plan for taxes and investments, and an internal bookkeeper, Katya, who reconciles the books. By reconcile I mean that she inputs all of the receipts into QuickBooks and then compares the actual expenses to the expected expenses. She then provides financial reports and a summary to me and Kevin, my co-founder, of how we're doing money-wise.

Katya is wonderful, she's been with me for years, and I trust her immensely. But she doesn't have access to the actual money. Only Kevin and I have access to the actual bank accounts. She has the ability to log in and download reports and data, but she cannot log in and spend money.

I've simply heard too many horror stories of founders who have walked away from the finances of the business only to get burned by an employee or accountant. Embezzlement comes in many forms. How do they embezzle?

An extra person, say the accountant's spouse who doesn't work for the company, can be added to payroll. I've read about that happening, even with a local company I'm familiar with. As the busy business owner, you may not even pay attention to how much payroll is or if it has recently increased.

Another means of embezzlement is when a check is written to a vendor who's in cahoots with the bookkeeper. They write the vendor a check from your account, you don't question it, and the payment gets split between the bookkeeper and the vendor. Think I'm paranoid? It happens more frequently than you may suspect.

Yet another way is simply for the accountant, employee, or bookkeeper to buy personal items on the company credit card. The expense goes to the company, but the item goes directly to them personally. You pay, they benefit, all without you knowing.

I've talked openly with Kevin and Katya about this risk. I've also reiterated that I trust Katya, and our accountants, immensely. But it's in my best interest, and definitely in theirs, for them to have limited access to the cash.

So I pay all the bills myself. Paying is easy since most bills are on autopay through my bank or on our American Express card. When I do have to individually pay bills, it's through my bank's online bill pay system, and it literally takes me only five minutes every two to three weeks.

I also receive the bank and credit card statements in the mail and review each transaction myself. We're still a small enough company where I can do that myself. I'm sure at some point that will need to change somehow, but for now, I review all expenses and ask for clarity when I see something I don't expect.

There's an added benefit to reviewing each expense ... I have the ability to spot and cut unnecessary expenses on a regular basis. Almost without exception, I find a service or two that we pay for but we don't leverage or need any more. When I suspect we can cut something, I'll reach out to whoever uses that service and confirm if we still need it. Sometimes the answer is "yes" but other times it's a resounding, "kind of."

In situations where we still use a service, but it's lost its novelty with us for whatever reason, I'll see if we can cut back on that service. Maybe we don't need the pro plan any more and the basic plan will work for us.

Are we really using all of the features of the pro plan, or can we drop down and save ten, thirty, or fifty dollars a month? If my team kind of, sort of, thinks that maybe the lower plan will work, I reduce our plan. I'd rather reduce the plan immediately if there's a question about it than continue to pay more and have lingering doubts.

It doesn't matter if it's three dollars a month or $300—I take whatever time I need to cut it. It can be a pain and sometimes time-consuming to discontinue a service. But even if it's not a lot of money, I still cut it. For expenses that we need, that will help us service our clients better or grow our business, I will spend the money, and sometimes lavishly.

But wasteful spending? I cut that ruthlessly.

Protect what you make. Put systems into place to ensure others don't take what's not theirs, and don't waste your money on services you don't need or use.

→ Accounting

It's important to separate your business finances from your personal finances. As a rule, avoid intermingling your personal and business finances. Also as a rule, you'll need to start tracking individual transactions for your business.

You have to keep clean financial records for your business since there are tax and audit implications. Since you'll be handling your business and personal finances separately, you can handle your personal finances however you want. That's a personal choice. The best way to start separating your personal and business finances is by using a separate bank account for business, and recording every deposit and withdrawal from that account. This is often referred to as keeping the books, or bookkeeping.

When tax time arrives, you'll need to subtract your business expenses from your revenue and pay taxes on your profits. In order to do that properly, you'll need to be able to document who each expense was paid to and categorize it (e.g., rent, software, subcontractors).

You could do this manually in a spreadsheet. That is, if you like doing things the hard way. Like other business problems, there are literally hundreds of solutions available that will make your life easier. In this case, an accounting solution like QuickBooks will be your best friend. Sign up for the lowest plan that you need and get started. I recommend using their online solution instead of the program that you download to your computer. It's cheap and effective.

When I was in charge of the back office for my wife's bakery, I kept the books myself. I did it all—entered transactions, reconciled bank statements, reconciled credit card statements, dealt with chargebacks from customers, ran payroll, and paid taxes. I was able to figure out how to be an accountant, on top of everything else I was doing, and I saved money by doing it myself. But I also sacrificed a lot of time and a little bit of sanity.

Although I still could keep the books myself, after that experience I realized that I never wanted to again. You know the saying that something is the last thing you want to do, or that something is on the bottom of your to-do list? Well, keeping the books wasn't even that high of a priority to me! When I was in charge of the books, I would always procrastinate until the last minute.

Payroll, as an example, must be filed by a certain date and time in order for direct deposit to happen. I was pretty good about that, but not perfect, and missed payroll once. Learn from my experience—never, ever think it'll be okay to miss payroll. Your employees expect to be paid on time, every time, and if you miss it like I did, there is no excuse whatsoever.

Other accounting tasks could be put off longer. Taxes, it turns out, don't actually have to be paid by the due date. It's a good idea to, and you'll get fined if you don't, but I found out that when I missed a tax due date, it was generally okay to pay late if I paid all the late fees. That meant unless I was on top of my accounting game, I'd miss some tax payments even though I had the money to make the payments.

The worst for me, though, was entering in every transaction into QuickBooks. It was time-consuming, tedious, and I frankly just hated it. A close second worst is reconciliation, which is when you get a monthly statement from your bank or credit card and have to check that every transaction in the statement is in your books. Wanting my books to be clean and perfect, I'd find myself spending an hour or more tracking down why I might be off by just a few pennies.

Having had enough of keeping my own books in the past, when I started my next business after the bakery, I swore I'd do things differently. I hired an accountant to take care of payroll and I quickly hired Katya to run the books. I kept the ability to log into QuickBooks so I could poke around at any time, and I received financial summaries on a regular basis. But I kept some financial aspects myself, such as receiving and depositing checks, transferring money between accounts, and having the ability to "touch" the money in our bank accounts.

As time has gone on, I've relinquished more accounting responsibilities. Katya now receives checks from clients in a PO box near her house in Florida, she deposits them remotely using our bank's mobile app, and she initiates our twice-a-month Profit First transfers. She even has access to our credit cards with the authority to purchase as needed and to allow others to spend as needed within a reasonable amount.

The last accounting function that I still retain is access to the money itself. Only Kevin, my co-founder, and I have the ability to withdraw money from the bank or to write checks. Although there's a lot of financial activity being initiated by others, I still watch the money and review bank and credit card statements every month. I still question individual transactions at times, and I'm still ensuring that we don't spend money frivolously.

When you're just starting out, be sure to start off on the right financial foot. Sign up for QuickBooks Online or a similar accounting package, and keep the books yourself at first. Doing so will teach you what needs to be done and what's important, but then aim to transition those functions to a bookkeeper. Try to get out of the day-to-day world of accounting and instead oversee what's happening with your finances. It'll free up your time and your sanity while ensuring that your money is kept track of properly.

→ Making payroll

Once you have employees, they will appreciate getting paid on a predictable basis!

Miss payroll, and it's a huge problem, and it's a symptom of a much bigger problem. Most companies miss payroll either because they can't afford to pay their employees, or they're just terribly unorganized.

When I co-owned the bakery with my wife, she handled operations and I handled the business end of things. She worked in the bakery full time while I continued with my day job and helped after hours and on weekends.

One of my clear responsibilities was payroll, and as I mentioned, I missed payroll once. I could make up dozens of excuses why I allowed that to happen, but the bottom line is that I was terribly unorganized at the time and didn't fully appreciate the impact it would have, not only on the employees, but on my wife. She called frantically that day, and in disbelief that I hadn't processed payroll.

She dropped everything, ran to the bank, and withdrew cash from our bank account to cover pay quickly. Although the employees got paid that day, it wasn't a good enough solution. I had caused irreparable damage.

Unfortunately for my wife, I learned a valuable lesson that day at her expense. It was a terrible mistake, greatly hurt employee morale, and it hurt our relationship for some time. I vowed that would never happen again.

When I later started my own company and hired my first employee, I hired a payroll accountant. Not only did this ensure that my employees would be paid on time, but it also took care of the other responsibilities I had as an employer.

Hiring a payroll accountant ensures that the proper taxes are withheld from paychecks, paid to the government on time, and all legal pay requirements are satisfied. A payroll accountant also ensures that my employees will get paid on time. I'm still accountable, but the payroll accountant is responsible to make it happen. Outsourcing payroll greatly reduced the risk of my employees not getting paid on time, and of payroll getting jacked up. As a positive side effect, it also freed me up from doing the research to ensure compliance with employment and tax laws and from the ongoing effort of processing payroll.

When you're ready to hire employees, do yourself a huge favor. Hire an accountant or payroll company to process your payroll. It is money well spent.

Besides being unorganized like I was at the bakery, another common reason that companies miss payroll is because they simply don't have enough cash on hand to pay their employees.

In some cases, it's because of cash flow issues. Most commonly a company is waiting for their customers to pay them so they have enough cash to cover payroll. This is an easy problem to solve by tightening up payment terms and ideally collecting payment upfront and automatically by ACH. But if the problem is more severe, like the company is chronically losing money, then the fundamental issue must be addressed.

To ensure we have enough cash on hand for payroll, we project the cash flow of our operating bank account (aka OPEX) every month. We project the revenue that will flow into that account and the expenses that will flow out. For each transaction, we project the running balance that should be in the account on that day. Payroll is simply another expense. With that, we can clearly project the balance of the operating account on a day-by-day basis for the next month.

What magical tool do we use to model our cash flow? It's actually quite sophisticated, but it's also quite ubiquitous. It's a common spreadsheet. In our case, we use Google Sheets, but you can use Excel or whatever spreadsheet tool you prefer.

We start by projecting the balance of the operating account at the beginning of the month. We then add a row for each injection of cash and for every expense—utilities, credit card payments, payroll and payroll taxes, and any others we anticipate. We also project when new revenue will flow into that bank account. With each row, the projected account balance increases or decreases depending on whether the line item is revenue or an expense.

We started doing this after getting one too many emails from our bank, letting us know that we had overdrawn our OPEX account yet again. When that happened, we'd temporarily move cash from other accounts into OPEX to cover the shortfall. We got by doing that, but it would put a pinch on other things such as paying taxes on time or building up a reserve. But when payroll is about to hit your bank account, you'd better make sure there's enough money there!

We needed a way to ensure we didn't run out of money and to ensure we always had enough to pay our employees on time.

The system of projecting cash flow works amazingly well, and I recommend you go through the budgeting exercise yourself. The first time Katya and I projected cash flow, it took us about two hours. Frankly, we didn't fully understand what all our expenses were and the timing of those expenses. But after projecting it once, it rapidly got easier and faster. The second time we projected expenses, it took us an hour. Now, after doing it for over two years, it takes about ten minutes.

One more thing to consider ... employee withholdings.

If an employee makes, say, $100,000 a year, then they won't actually take home $100,000. They'll take home less because you'll withhold taxes and other items such as their portion of their health insurance premium. You'll hold onto those withholdings, but then will later have to pay those withholdings to the health insurance company or pay those taxes to the government.

You're just holding onto those funds temporarily. Don't forget about them when you project cash flow! That's a common mistake that new entrepreneurs make—they cover payroll, but then fail to have enough money to cover the withholdings that have to get paid to the government and other benefits providers. Ensure you have enough for it all.

→ Pay frequency

We started projecting our cash flow because of an anomaly in our finances that we picked up on. But it took a year or two to see the pattern and understand why the anomaly was happening. Bear with me as I go into the finer details of the financial anomaly. It just might save you from the same trouble I had.

Every few months, we'd have what appeared to be a really bad month. Nothing significant had happened to decrease our revenue, but our profitability for the month would drop or go negative. It was frustrating and didn't make sense, until we figured out it had to do with payroll.

You will pay your employees on a frequency that you decide. The most common frequencies are weekly, every other week, or twice a month.

At one of my first jobs, I was paid twice a month, on the first and the fifteenth. Because each month has a different number of days, one of the paychecks I received would be for the same amount every month. But the other would be for more or less, depending on how many days there were at the tail end of the previous month. As the employee receiving the pay, I realized that one of my checks would be slightly bigger than the other, but I wasn't able to predict by how much.

When it was time for me to pick the pay frequency for my employees, I knew I didn't want a variable model like I had previously experienced. So I went with paying employees every other week. That provided a consistent stream of income to our employees, made pay periods consistent, and was a frequency I was familiar with. But that turned into the cash flow problem we discovered in the operating bank account.

With fifty-two weeks in a year, paying every other week will result in twenty-six paydays per year. That results in getting two paychecks per month for ten out of twelve months a year, and getting a third paycheck for two out of twelve months.

That third paycheck, although it's quite obvious to see in retrospect, was giving our cash flow convulsions. Although we were operating business as usual, the wages we paid during those two months were 50 percent higher than in other months. When looking at profit and loss over a calendar month, those increased wages destroyed our profits for the month.

Once we realized this was happening, which took much longer than you would suspect, we started to track the cash flow of the operating account, modeling every expected expense and deposit. If we were going to have variable months, then I wanted to know about it before payday. We could not risk running out of money on payday.

Every other financial transaction we had, whether it was invoicing or paying bills, was on a monthly frequency. Having this one expense being variable, and dependent on the month of the year, was a real problem. If we lost money one month, was it because of the third payroll or because of other reasons? It was easy to see when the third payroll hit our account, but it wasn't as easy to exclude that from the profit and loss statements to analyze how we did otherwise.

Since accounting is done on a monthly, quarterly, and annual basis, only some of those reports would work for us. The monthly reports were almost worthless. They showed we had terrible months for two months of the year, but financial reports were also incorrectly positive for the other ten months of the year because the actual payroll expense for the month was artificially low, since some payroll for that month was paid in the other two months when we experienced a third payday. Even the quarterly reports were messy because two quarters had an extra payroll, and two quarters did not. That meant that only the annual accounting reports were accurate.

Once the problem was discovered, I instantly knew we had to fix it. One way to fix it was to change our reporting periods from the monthly, quarterly, and annual reports to periods of time that correlated with pay periods. One business owner I know accounts for this anomaly by running "monthly" reports that span two, two-week pay periods. So his reporting runs in twenty-eight-day cycles, but those cycles do not correlate with a calendar month.

That means that his "monthly" reports will often span different months and quarters. There's no asking for the "January" report, as an example. You'd have to ask for the "January 6th to February 3rd" report. By the way, leap years will ensure that the dates of these so-called payroll months don't line up consistently year after year.

That's just too complicated. As modern humans, we naturally group time into months, quarters, and years. I didn't want to invent some other measure of time just because we pay our employees every other week. It seemed like paying twice a month would help. In my experience at a previous job, the second paycheck per month would be a variable amount. Although that minimized the variability that I was currently experiencing with the third paycheck per month, it didn't entirely remove that variability. It was close, but not exactly the solution I sought. Why did this need to be so complicated?

Then I thought, *What if we paid twice a month regardless of the number of days per month?* That would result in twenty-four paydays per year, and each pay would be for the same amount. So if someone makes $100,000 a year, then their pay would be $100,000 / 24 = $4,166.67, before taxes, each payday. That solution was effective, but would it work for employees?

The downside for the company doing this was that during short months, say, February, the employee would take home more than they technically earned. Although that would probably seem like a win to employees, in my mind it was a negative. But it was also countered by the fact that in longer months, they'd take home a little less than "earned."

We let the employees know of the problem and asked if they'd suffer a hardship by getting paid more regularly and by not having the surprise third payday a month. The reality is that the third payday came close to the end of the month every time, and employees barely recognized it was happening. It just wasn't an issue for them, but it was for the company.

The calendar is complicated, but payroll shouldn't be. In the end, we decided to proceed with paying everyone 1/24 of their annual pay, twice a month.

Transitioning required careful coordination with employees and with our payroll accountants. We planned for it many weeks in advance and postponed the rollout when we projected an issue. Everyone was well-aware of the plan, and when the appointed payday came to cutover, it went flawlessly.

Ever since that transition to paying twice a month, where each pay is 1/24 of annual pay, everything has worked out great. Our books instantly snapped to, and we could much better project cash flow. Finally, we had a pay frequency that worked just as well for the company as it did for the employees.

If you haven't yet selected a pay frequency, I strongly recommend twice per month and in equal amounts.

If you already have a pay frequency in place and want to solve your reporting problem, then you now have a way forward. But if you don't want to, or can't, change your frequency, then you'd better come up with a reporting mechanism besides calendar months, so it's clear to you exactly how the business is running regardless of pay frequencies.

→ Credit cards

Credit cards are great because when you buy something, you don't have to part with your cash for at least another month when the next monthly payment is due. Delaying your cash payments helps with cash flow because your cash stays in your bank account for longer than if you parted with your cash at the time of the purchase.

But using a credit card is also a risk. If you don't pay off your credit card each month and carry a balance, then you will pay a lot in interest. You also run the risk of not paying on time each month and being hit with late fees.

If you're running a service-based business like mine, then hopefully your expenses will start off low and you won't need to spend much money. If you're opening a retail spot, you'll be spending plenty, but in that case, you'll probably want a proper business loan rather than relying on credit cards and their high fees if you need to carry a balance.

When I opened my business, I used a debit card for everything. When I spent money, it came directly out of my business checking account. It was a simple arrangement and ensured I never got myself into financial trouble, because I could only spend what I had in the bank. I kept with that system for many years and only recently switched to using an American Express card to earn travel points.

In my business, there's a fair amount of pass-through revenue— money we collect from our clients to buy ads online. That money gets deposited into our bank account and then spent on ads in places like Google and Facebook. We paid those ads with a debit card as well.

When I realized I could earn travel points if I bought those ads with an American Express card instead of our debit card, I was still hesitant to switch. There's a comfort in knowing that you can never overspend when using a debit card. But once I came to grips with the fact that I could earn tens of thousands of points or more a month simply by changing my payment method, we switched to paying with an American Express. Plus, if I wanted to, I could pay the American Express balance off frequently, even daily if I really wanted to, so I couldn't get myself into financial trouble.

I don't travel a lot, but when I do, I'd prefer to not have to pay for it. When I use the American Express to pay for online ads, I end up getting points even though the money is literally just passing through my books. Doing so results in hundreds of thousands of travel points generated every year. The amount of points will increase as our business, and pass-through funds, also grows.

Another perk of the American Express card is that we can pick a spending category that gives us three times the points. The category we picked was advertising, which amplifies the effect of getting points for pass-through dollars even more. That means that if we buy $100,000 of advertising online in a month, then we earn 300,000 points that month. That adds up fast.

With all of those American Express points adding up, I can now travel for free. Not only is that pretty cool, but it gives you a competitive advantage. How so? Imagine if you wanted to go to a conference or wanted to meet a prospect who was out of town. If you had to pay for the airfare and hotel, it could cost you thousands of dollars each time. That's enough money for you to second-guess if you should travel. But if you can travel for free, then all you're sacrificing is your time away from home. Without the financial burden of travel, you'll be more likely to travel and more likely to benefit from situations that others without travel points will let pass up.

So travel points can be great, especially if you have pass-through revenue. If the money is flowing through your books, then you might as well get something out of it.

Here's the important part, though. Credit cards are great for cash flow and for the perks, but don't carry a balance. Just like with your personal finances, be smart with your business finances. If you carry a balance, you will pay a hefty fee. Yes, I've done it a few times when cash was tight, but I hated it and worked hard to pay it down. If you find yourself in a situation where you can't pay the whole bill off each month, then come up with a plan on how you'll pay it off over a set number of months.

I recommend that you hold off on getting a business credit card until your business is stable. Use debit cards until then. It just makes things easier, and in the beginning of your entrepreneurial journey, you will have other worries besides maximizing the travel points you can earn. Simplify everything you can at first, and defer complexity for later.

Chapter takeaways

1. Raising capital takes your focus away from your business. Consider refocusing exclusively on validating your idea by finding people who will buy what you're selling.
2. If you're not sure what you would do if you raised capital, then skip that step altogether and focus on growing your business.
3. Although business license taxes are based on your top-line revenue, most other business taxes are based on your profit.
4. One strategy to lowering your taxes is to reinvest your profits back into the business. You can hire more employees, buy advertising, and use those funds before the end of the year, which will increase your expenses, lower your profits, and lower your tax bill. But don't be wasteful—only do this for legit business investments.
5. Look into Profit First—a book and system for organizing your money into different categories. This simple system helps you know when you need to lower your expenses in order to maintain other important parts of your finances, like paying yourself, paying taxes, and ensuring you make a profit.
6. Keep a close eye on your expenses. Personally review every transaction on your credit card and bank statements. Do this every month.
7. Question whether you really need a service. If you can lower or cut the service, and thus the expense, do it.
8. Make sure you always pay employees on time. Miss payroll, and employees will have legitimate reasons to question your financial stability and whether yours is the right business for them to be in.
9. Missing payroll is often caused by lack of funds on payday. Reduce your clients' payment terms as much as possible. Instead of offering Net 30, offer Net 7. Ideally, don't even offer Net terms, and instead bill them at the beginning of the month using ACH or their credit card.

10. Don't ever "borrow" from employee withholdings. Put the employee tax payments that you withhold from their paychecks into a separate bank account. That's not your money to borrow. Consider that the government's money.
11. Consider paying your employees twice a month in equal payments of 1/24th of their annual salary. Paying on other frequencies, such as every other week, will skew your monthly financial reports to the point where you may not know exactly how much profit or loss you really made.
12. Don't intermingle personal and business funds. All business funds, both revenue and expenses, should flow through your business bank account.
13. When you start your company, use a debit card for expenses. It'll be harder to get yourself into financial trouble if you can only spend what's in your bank account.
14. With time, consider putting expenses on a credit card. Not only do you defer paying for items you buy, you can earn travel points, or enjoy other benefits, by purchasing with a credit card. But beware—always pay off your credit card on time, otherwise late fees and interest can get expensive.

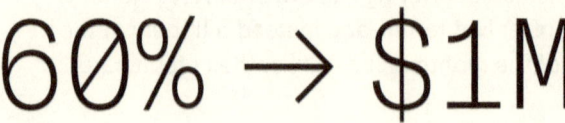

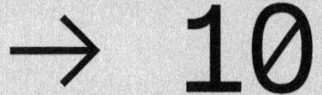 10

Hiring and firing

You can go it alone or with others. Like everything in life, there are pros and cons to each way of doing things.

From the beginning, I knew I wanted to build a team. I knew that would also mean personnel issues and drama, and there have been many. Many entrepreneurs don't want to deal with the messiness of human resources.

But the downsides of managing people are offset by massive upsides in overall productivity, the ability to specialize, the ability to land bigger and better clients, and the sheer amount of brainpower you can put toward growing your business.

→ Hiring your first employee

While I was still employed full time, I picked up freelancing. For the last six months of employment, before I went all-in and started working full time for myself, the freelancing consumed pretty much every free moment I had after working a full schedule. I thought that once I quit my day job, I'd have way more free time since I could freelance during the day instead of on nights and weekends.

What I found was that once I was free from corporate life, I still didn't have a lot of free time. I continued to work pretty much every waking hour. This went on through the first winter and into the spring. By early summer, still working ridiculously crazy, I was about halfway through a good-sized project when another big project was awarded to me.

I wanted the work. I needed the work. But I was already working my ass off and knew that it wasn't enough. I had to finish one project, move on to the next project, and keep looking for the next one after that to ensure my pipeline didn't run dry. I still had basic tasks to take care of in the business, like finishing my website and putting together a marketing plan.

Up to that point, all of the work I got was from Elance and from tapping my personal network. I had yet to put in the hard work of finding more clients beyond that. I wanted to grow the company, but couldn't while I was wrapped up in these projects.

I had tinkered with hiring other freelancers. They could be helpful, but they weren't exactly what I was looking for. For starters, they were more expensive than I wanted to pay. As a freelancer, your goal is to charge as much as possible per client because you typically work on short-duration projects and maybe only once every few weeks. I was freelancing myself and knew that game well. Often, a freelancer would want almost as much from me as I was getting paid by my client.

With most freelancers I hired, the margin between what I was getting paid by my client and what I paid the freelancer was sometimes only five dollars an hour. Sure, that could add up if I had a slew of freelancers, but in reality, my freelancers were only billing twenty to forty hours a week. Although I could make $100 to $200 a week off of them, it just didn't add up to enough profits, and I still had all the problems that came with managing projects and people.

Also with freelancers, I was never quite satisfied with their level of commitment. Their scope of work had to be pretty rigidly defined; otherwise, the costs could get out of hand quickly. If I wanted a fixed scope and fixed price agreement with a freelancer, it would take me time to figure out the scope.

Defining the perfect scope for a freelancer would take more time than I wanted to spend on it. If it wasn't perfectly defined, then I was opening myself up to costly change orders. If I hired them by the hour, the work would mysteriously seem to take longer than I thought it should. They didn't seem committed to doing amazing work or to solving the clients' problems, just to making money.

What I realized was that I expected a higher level of commitment from the people I was bringing on to work with me. But it was an unrealistic expectation to put on freelancers, especially those who had day jobs and were moonlighting after hours.

How could I expect a full commitment from them when I was keeping them at arm's length with a freelancing gig? Why should I expect them to commit to me when I wasn't fully committing to them?

That's when I decided I needed to hire a full-time employee.

Having the security of a new project under contract, and the future revenue it would provide, I quickly calculated that I had enough coming my way to pay me and someone else. But the revenue I expected would only pay us both for about six months. Beyond that, I'd have to go find more work. That is, if my calculations were right in the first place!

In a perfect world, you'd have enough money in the bank to pay for you and your employees for years, even if no new revenue came in. But it would take years, maybe decades, to save up that much. You simply cannot wait that long before you start growing your company. Taking some risk is required if you want to grow your company.

I had never hired someone before, at least not for a company where I was the sole owner, and everything rested on my shoulders. It was nerve-wracking for sure. I went about trying to find someone on the cheap. I drafted a job description and posted it on Craigslist and in a local group forum.

Interviewing only a couple of people, I luckily happened upon someone who was a fit. She didn't have a ton of formal experience, and most of it came from working on volunteer projects that benefited the community and local cities. Her experience was also quite varied, having dabbled in different frameworks and systems, but not mastering any of them.

The interview went well. We clicked. Her husband was in the military, so she didn't need health insurance. That was a relief to me because I hadn't yet looked into what it would take to provide health insurance to employees, but I was sure it would be a pain to set up and would be expensive. Later I'd find out that I was right, but at that time, I was able to avoid that pain.

Salary-wise, she was spot on with the amount of pay I had in mind. I'm sure she's making double or triple that now, but at the time, it was a good fit for both of us. She needed the formal experience, and I needed her contribution.

Speaking with my wife after the interview, I told her that I would make sure my new hire would always get paid on time, no matter what. I was fully committed to making that happen come hell or high water.

But me? I wasn't totally confident there'd always be enough left over for me. I had done the rough calculations, and everything looked like it would work, but so many variables can affect cash flow.

If we didn't finish a deliverable as fast as I expected, then we'd be delayed in invoicing. If the client delayed in paying, then the cash wouldn't be there. Shoot, if the client canceled the project, I would be screwed. What if one of our laptops blew up, and I needed to drop another couple thousand for a high-end MacBook Pro? I still wasn't even clear about my tax situation as a new business owner. There were a lot of variables, and I didn't have all the answers.

In the end, I pulled the trigger and hired her. But it was the hardest decision I've made to date as a business owner. When you decide to hire someone, and when they entrust their livelihood to you, that's a real commitment. And it wasn't just a financial commitment. It's their career, too, and I was about to be responsible for her career development. Hiring is a huge responsibility and one you should not rush into.

In the end, everything worked out great. I was able to pay her and myself without fail. We didn't encounter any major issues with the projects or the clients, and I continued to find new projects to backfill our work pipeline as we finished projects.

In retrospect, I would say that I lucked out on my first hire. A lot could have gone wrong.

More recently, we've enhanced the way we go about hiring new employees. We don't advertise on Craigslist anymore and instead post jobs on Indeed and LinkedIn. We can find better candidates there. We also have a more rigorous interview process consisting of multiple rounds of interviews with different staff. We run background checks and call references.

Over time, your hiring practices will become more sophisticated too. But for your first hire, you just need to trust your gut. Advertise for the job and keep interviewing people until you find the person who you think has the skills you need and the work ethic to help you get your business off the ground.

→ Continuing to build the team

Demand for our services continued to be strong. As more projects rolled in, I found myself yet again needing more help. I already had one full-time employee who was busy on a project, but I needed someone else to take on a new project. Rationalizing that one full-time employee was probably enough of a commitment for the time being, I once again tried the freelancer route.

After interviewing a few candidates, I found someone who seemed to be a fit for a project that was about to start. He interviewed well and had the skills I needed for the project. I agreed to his hourly rate and sent him the freelancing agreement. He signed the papers, returned them quickly, and I gave him access to the systems he needed to get the work done. Everything was in place, and he knew what needed to be done.

And then ... nothing.

Although he was Johnny On The Spot during the interview and onboarding process, I guess he just wasn't interested in working. He never did anything else and never returned my emails. I'd call and leave voicemails, but he never returned those either. After a couple of weeks, I gave up on him. Execution, it seems, just wasn't in him.

I hired another freelancer who did a half-ass job and never finished. I ended up having to finish out that project, which just added to my stress level and extended the already twelve-hour days I was putting in at the time.

Having wasted enough time trying to augment my small staff with more freelancers, and remembering the previous lesson I learned about needing to commit to full-time employees, I decided it was time to hire another full-time person.

At about the same time, two opportunities came my way. A programmer I already knew asked if I knew anyone who was hiring. I was also asked by a prospect if I had anyone on staff who could work from his office about thirty hours a week. I thought I could hire the programmer, have him work most of the time at the prospect's office, and use that extra ten hours a week of his time to help me with other projects. Having never tried staff augmentation before, where you send your employee to the client's office to work on their projects every day, it seemed like it could be a sweet business model for us.

I hired the programmer and had him reporting to the client's office within a week. Although there was a financial upside to it, there was little chemistry with this new arrangement.

My first employee and I worked in the office side by side on a daily basis. We were in lockstep with each other, but our third employee worked thirty minutes away on a completely different kind of project. Those extra ten hours a week I thought the third employee would have to help us out on other projects never materialized, so we rarely worked on anything together. Not working together and not seeing each other much, we had little in common. We were less a team and more a collection of freelancers.

Not recognizing this fault yet, and thinking that maybe staff augmentation was the model I wanted for the company, I pursued more staff augmentation contracts. We landed a $10,000/month agreement with a local startup that badly needed our help. They lacked expertise in project management, a skill I personally was highly capable of providing.

This meant a lot of my time, upward of 90 percent every week, would be devoted to my client and growing his business. While I spent most of my time at the new client's office, my first employee worked by herself in our office or she'd work from home, and my second employee was at his client's office. We were spread all over the place and only touched base when needed. Although we were generating revenue, we had no sense of team at all.

As this most recent client's business grew, he needed more from us, and I continued to hire based on his demand. At our peak, we had five employees there day in and day out. I continued to spend a lot of time on that project, since he was our biggest client at the time.

→ **Creating a sense of team**

Our company finances were good, but this wasn't what I had in mind for company culture. People working for one client had nothing in common with people working for another client. The projects and industries were all different, so we rarely could help each other out if someone was on another project. Quickly, our employees began to form affinities with their clients' companies, instead of with our company.

I had a culture problem for sure and knew I needed to do something about it.

In order to get everyone together, at least for a little bit, I started organizing company lunches. Regardless of where someone worked on a daily basis, I asked them to come to our office, and we'd all go out to eat on the company's dime.

At first it was an excuse for everyone to get a free lunch and not much more than that. But I was surprised when people would tell me how much they looked forward to the company lunch. They could let their hair down a bit, reconnect with co-workers, and tell war stories about their projects and clients. Initially, I held the company lunches monthly, but quickly changed the frequency to every two weeks.

It became such a good experience that we continue the tradition to this day. Every two weeks, we hold a company lunch at our main office, as well as at remote locations where there are two or more employees in proximity to each other.

Wanting to continue to get our employees together and away from the daily grind of working on our clients' projects, I signed us all up to attend a conference. I was looking forward to taking the whole team, five of us by then, for a couple of days of learning, relaxing, and bonding.

We booked flights for everyone, and we were off for a few days to Knoxville. It was an all-expenses-paid trip for everyone. Wining, dining, everything was included. We attended a lot of great sessions and spent a lot of time together. Since we were gone for a few days, the billable time stopped. Between the expenses and the lack of billable time, it wasn't a cheap trip. But it was great to get everyone together.

As fun as the trip was and as much as it boosted morale, it didn't quite hit the mark when it came to education. Different people have different ways of learning. At the time, I learned best from conferences and from books. Others in the company learned best from videos. Most of my folks were shy and weren't comfortable being around a big group of people. Conferences, it turned out, weren't really their jam.

What I thought was a great perk—going on an annual trip for an all-expenses-paid conference—wasn't what everyone else wanted. Sensing that and getting direct feedback from a few people, I decided to forgo the trip the next year.

Still wanting to provide a great learning environment, I worked with each employee to identify what they wanted to learn and how they learned best. One employee learned best by working on projects and requested three days of paid time off so he could teach himself a new skill that I needed someone in the company to learn. Another person wanted a membership to educational videos, and another just wanted a few books a year. All of these solutions worked great. I found that it's best to let people learn the way they want to learn instead of forcing a "perk" on them.

I continued to try to find ways to build up the team. Another system I created was the kudos system. The idea was to foster a sense of collaboration in the team. If someone helped you on a project or a problem you were wrestling with, then you could give them "kudos" through our online chat program.

Each person was granted twenty kudos points per week to award to anyone else on the team. They could award one point at a time, or all twenty at once to one person. It was up to each person to award their points as they deemed fit.

The person who was awarded the most kudos by their peers each month was awarded a $300 bonus. For the first year or so, I would hand out the bonus in cash. I found that handing someone $300 cash and recognizing them for their contribution in person had a big impact. That impact was amplified when I did it in front of the rest of the team, so I tried to award the bonus at one of our company lunches. The winner still had to pay taxes on the $300 cash bonus, but it was great to get that bonus in hand.

As the team grew and we gained remote workers, paying in cash stopped being feasible. The accountants got confused by my cash withdrawals, and I could only award cash to local people, so we ended up simply adding it to the winner's paycheck. But we still try to make the announcement a big deal, announcing the winner in front of the whole company during one of our all-hands meetings.

We've also modified the kudos system so that people can be recognized for contributions beyond just helping each other out. We eventually expanded the reasons for awarding kudos to be in line with our core values. Now we have to identify which core value the person has demonstrated in order for points to be awarded.

Whether you work on it or not, your company will have a culture. But if you don't focus on it and shape it, it could end up being a culture that you don't like.

If you find yourself in a situation where you're not happy with the way people are working together, then it's important to put practices into place to create the culture that you desire. You could follow my lead and start holding company lunches or create a system for your staff to reward each other. Most important, though, is to ensure that people get to know each other and show appreciation for working together.

Although I didn't fully understand it at the time, culture is more than simply getting everyone together and creating "feel good" programs. It's important that everyone adhere to a similar set of principles in how they go about their work. I was about to learn this the hard way.

→ Firing

Firing someone sucks. No one likes to do it, and the first time you fire someone, it feels terrible.

I never want to fire someone. But I need to have the right people doing the right things for the company. When it's clear that someone just isn't a fit, you owe it to yourself, to them, and to the rest of your company to release them.

My first firing was anything but the textbook version of the right way to fire someone. But I'm going to share that experience now. Like the rest of *Million Dollar Journey*, I want you to learn from my mistakes, so when you encounter a similar situation, you'll be better prepared.

One of my clients reached out to me directly. At the time, we were still experimenting with the staff augmentation model, and my employee worked out of the client's office on a daily basis. My client grumbled that my guy just wasn't cutting it, and my client didn't want to spend any more of his budget on the employee. I went to the client's office to try to figure out what was going on and to see if I could salvage the situation. It wasn't so much a budget problem as he had little faith in my employee's ability to do the work.

My employee was surprised when the client cut him. He attributed the cut to financial constraints, and I just didn't have the stomach to tell him the truth. I kept that information to myself and started to have my employee work out of our office.

I didn't have anything in particular for him to work on, so I gave him random tasks for a bit until I figured things out. I felt compelled to keep him employed, even though the reason I hired him was to work the staff augmentation contract which, it turned out, he wasn't a fit for.

His work, I found out once he was in the office full time, wasn't the best. Week after week, I'd ask for progress updates, and he'd tell me he was almost done. But over and over, he didn't complete work on time, and the quality of his work was subpar. I began to compensate for him and would jump in to finish his projects.

He was relieved every time I jumped in to finish his projects, but I resented it. To spare hurting his feelings, I didn't say much about how I was feeling, but I was building up a case in my mind for firing him.

Quickly I realized that there were fewer tasks that I could assign to him. After another epic failure and having run out of work I trusted to give him, it was time to have "the talk." I dreaded it, but it had to be done.

We met face to face, and I explained the issues I was having with him. It was a terrible meeting. He was surprised. He was confused. I can understand why, since it was the first time I had been totally transparent about his issues and their impact. I told him it just wasn't working out.

We couldn't keep going on like this. It wasn't good for him, it wasn't good for me, and it wasn't good for the company. I let him go.

I wasn't happy with the way it went down. Looking back, I realized that I had been too passive when issues came up. I had sheltered him from too many of the problems that he was causing.

I learned that I owe it to employees to let them know about issues as they arise. It's no fun to tell your employee that a client isn't happy with them or that you're unhappy about something, but there's a learning opportunity that is unfair to keep from them. I had to be fully transparent.

I walked away from that first firing having learned a few valuable lessons.

- → Never keep bad news from employees. They need that feedback so they can course correct before it snowballs out of control.
- → I should not have to fix problems that my employees create. Of course I'll help them, but that should be the exception and not the norm.
- → Staff augmentation wasn't for me. A hands-off approach with my employees is not what I wanted.
- → Although he wasn't a fit, I had yet to articulate to the company what I expected of our employees and of myself. I wanted us to act, and in some cases, not act, in certain ways. What I took as assumptions, I had yet to communicate effectively to the team.

Chapter takeaways

1. You can only scale so much as a solopreneur. In order to grow your business, you're going to need to hire people.
2. Hiring is a huge responsibility. As the employer, you become not only responsible for your employees' financial well-being, but also for their careers.
3. Create a sense of team. Get everyone together for lunches, happy hours, video calls, or other ways for everyone to get to know each other.
4. Provide learning opportunities. This allows employees to get better at what they do and, in turn, they'll perform better on the job.
5. If an employee is not a fit, be honest. Let them know early and often about your concerns. Don't let them be surprised if you have to fire them.

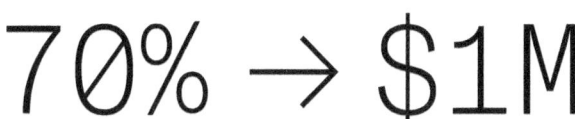

70% → $1M

→ 11

Developing your people

→ Core values

After my first firing experience, I knew that I needed to write down expectations of how I wanted our staff to act and interact with each other. Our company lacked core values.

Core values are a communal belief system for your company. They are a handful of expectations, typically determined by the founder or leader of the company, and put into place to guide the company's actions and decisions.

Once defined, you need to do more than just have them printed and hanging on the wall. You need to live by each and every core value. As the leader of your company, it's of utmost importance that you lead by example and find ways to keep core values in front of the entire team. Core values are a reflection of you, and if you don't live up to one of them, you will be viewed as a hypocrite, and your core values will be a joke.

Only people who you believe exhibit your core values should make it through the interview process, receive an offer letter, and remain with your company.

Conversely, you should fire people who don't live by your core values. Core values are uncompromising. You cannot allow someone to work at your company who doesn't exhibit your core values on an ongoing basis. I'm not saying to fire someone the first time they don't exhibit a core value, but they should be warned and fired if they continue to not live by these values.

It is your responsibility to weave these values into everything you do, every moment of every day. Find opportunities to reinforce your core values. The kudos system we use at Array Digital does just that on a daily basis. An employee can give another employee kudos points for exhibiting one or more core values.

Shortly after that first firing, I took a stab at drafting our first few core values. Once published, I spoke about them often. As I continued to refer to the first draft of the core values, I realized that, in some cases, what I wrote was slightly different than what I intended. Each time I noticed a discrepancy, I'd update the core values to get them a little bit closer to what I believed.

Like most areas of business, core values should be an iterative process. It's okay to improve them over time. Be sure to communicate each time you make a change, and explain your rationale for the change, so your employees are in sync with the updated set of core values.

But I worried that by setting my expectations and hiring and firing by core values, I would have a hard time finding and keeping employees. Was it worth the risk?

Yes!

This is where the mettle of a leader comes into play. You need to be strong, state what you believe, write it down, and communicate your core beliefs. You, and only you, can set the core values for your company. You can, and should, receive feedback from others in your company, but the core values must not be compromised.

The first version of our core values included honesty, learning, technical excellence, collaboration, transparency, timeliness, informal professionalism, and early adoption. I included a short narrative about each value. Each of those original core values has been morphed, clarified, combined, or removed as we've grown as a company and examined each and every core value.

I'm not suggesting that you haphazardly change your core values. Not in the least. Changing your core values is a big deal and you should only do it after careful examination. As the company grew, we learned more about who we were and who we wanted to become. When we changed our business model to focus on digital marketing, we updated our core values.

Here are the core values we currently live by today ...

Transparency

Being honest, and operating in a way that it is easy for others to see what actions are performed, are the bedrock for building trust with team members and clients. We will also be transparent with each other and our clients.

Quality

We are some of the best at what we do. We provide the highest quality offering practicable. We will always produce to a level that the majority of us believe is superior. Mediocre performance is unacceptable. Every team member is expected to highlight and address low quality work.

Urgency
Being on time is not enough. We must have a sense of urgency and complete our work as quickly as possible. We are growing fast, and there's no opportunity for downtime. The faster we are, the more we will accomplish in the same amount of time.

Winning
We are a winning organization. We win on a daily basis through our actions and attitudes. We win attention, mindshare, and business in the marketplace. We position our clients to win through our high quality, attention getting, digital marketing. We are in this to win it.

Passion
We are passionate about the work we do and how we do it. That passion can clearly be seen in the way we continuously learn more about our craft, in how we constantly strive to improve ourselves as individuals and as an organization, in how we carry ourselves professionally in all situations, and in how we are ready and willing to help a team member in need of assistance.

Some of the changes from the original core values are subtle, but important. As an example, the original expectation of Timeliness has changed to Urgency. We chronically completed our projects late when I first wrote our core values. I hated that we often didn't adhere to timelines and knew it was a major problem. First and foremost, I wanted to stop being late.

That's where Timeliness came into play. It was intended to correct the expectation that it was okay for us to be late, and to communicate that being on time was now expected. Going from late to on time was a huge improvement. But once we regularly delivered on time, I realized that we were undershooting ... we really needed to deliver as fast as we could. We had to raise the bar, and with that, we had to update the core value.

Sooner rather than later, write down what you believe to be your core values. Like I did, it's okay if you change them as time goes on. But you must believe in them. Unlike what I did, I recommend that you create your core values before you hire your first employee, and certainly before you fire someone.

→ Employee benefits

Perks. Everybody loves perks. But not everybody gets them. Also known as employee benefits, they are a form of compensation in addition to an employee's pay.

Examples of perks are:

- Paid time off (vacation)
- Sick leave
- Health insurance
- Life insurance
- Short-term disability insurance
- Long-term disability insurance
- Dental insurance
- Vision insurance
- Retirement plan, optionally with a company contribution
- Expense account
- Phone allowance
- Car allowance
- Tuition reimbursement
- Gym membership
- Childcare
- Free food/lunch

That's just a short list. When it comes to benefits, it's entirely up to you to be as extravagant as you want. The more difficult it is for an industry to find and retain employees, and if their profit margins allow, the more extravagant a company's benefits usually will be.

If you hire someone as a freelancer, contractor, or vendor, then the only compensation you are required to provide them is their pay. They are responsible for paying their own taxes and providing whatever benefits they want. You may provide them some benefits, but that's entirely up to you. An example may be paying for a contractor's parking fee if your office is in the city. But it would be rare for a company to pay for a contractor's time off or for their health insurance. Those types of more expensive perks are reserved for employees, and typically full-time employees at that.

With my first employee, I knew I had to provide some benefits. But benefits can be expensive. As a young company and hiring my first employee, I needed to keep my costs down as much as possible. What I needed was a minimal viable benefits package—just the absolute basics.

My first employee did not need health insurance or any other form of insurance. Her husband was in the military, and they provided health insurance to them both. It was a financial and logistical relief for me to not have to worry about health insurance. I didn't know how much health insurance would cost, but I knew it wouldn't be cheap. I also didn't know how to go about getting it, but I knew it would require research and consume a lot of my time to figure it out. Since she didn't need it, I could simply defer that research project for the time being.

She didn't need a computer from me either. I'd eventually buy her a company laptop, but when she was hired on, she opted to use her own. That was fine by me. High-end laptops are expensive, and I preferred to not have to buy one if I didn't have to. Although she provided the laptop, I bought an external monitor and a few small accessories for her to use. Those didn't cost much.

The big perk that I offered her was paid time off. I followed my last employer's paid time off model and offered comprehensive leave. With comprehensive leave, an employee can take time off, and get paid for it, for any reason whatsoever. They can use their paid time off for a vacation, when they're sick, or for a holiday. It's a nice system because, as the employer, I don't care why they're taking off, but I do need a predictable way of knowing how much time they'll take off and when they'll be gone.

So she got comprehensive leave instead of a set number of days off for vacation, another number for sick days, and another number of days for pre-defined holidays. Since comprehensive leave covers all the different types of leave, I offered four weeks of it. So 4 weeks × 5 days/week = 20 days of paid leave per year. That was twenty days that I was going to pay her, but she wasn't going to work.

The other formal perk I provided was to pay for her parking. My first office was in a downtown area, and it cost eighty-five dollars a month for a parking pass to the nearby garage. Not a ton of money, but it was one of those expenses that I assumed would aggravate an employee over time. So I picked up that expense and paid it directly.

That was my entire benefits package at first: comprehensive leave, free parking, and computer accessories. From a financial and logistical perspective, it was quite manageable. I also offered intangible perks, such as learning opportunities on and off the clock and the annual conferences we attended on my dime. Although my benefits package was simple, I also realized it wouldn't always be that way.

As we grew, I knew I wouldn't continue to luck out and find candidates who didn't need health insurance. I knew health insurance would be the next big perk I had to offer, since so many in the workforce need it. To start attracting the right kind of talent, I had to offer health insurance. That was the second big perk I added after comprehensive leave.

With my second employee, I offered a health insurance benefit. I'd yet to line up a plan and told him I was going to stand up a group health insurance plan soon. When he accepted the offer, I had to scramble to line up a plan. Talk about just-in-time benefits!

A friend of mine referred me to a health insurance broker. It was a relief to meet with the broker because there are countless insurance companies, all with their own plans and differing costs and benefits. We sat down, he asked me a few questions, and then he laid out several options with recommendations.

Here's an oversimplification of how health insurance plans work. You can choose from different plans with varying benefits and costs. Plans with more benefits will cost you a higher monthly premium than plans with less benefits. To pick the right plan for you, you need to consider the cost of your monthly premium and how much coverage you think you'll need.

I was going to enroll myself into the plan, too, so it needed to be a plan good enough for my family. I also needed a plan that would attract new employees, so I opted for a plan closer to the "Cadillac" plan —a plan that offered more benefits, but also a higher premium than other plans. After lining everything up with the health insurance broker, it was time for individuals to sign up. The company would pay for 50 percent of not only the employee's premium, but also 50 percent of the premium for their spouse and children.

In the long run, splitting the cost of the plan with employees turned out to be a good decision. If I were to offer health insurance at no cost, then employees likely wouldn't appreciate the value we provided. If it cost them nothing, then why not insist on the best health insurance plan that money can buy?

By splitting the cost with the employees, I found that they and I became partners over time in picking the right plan—one that balanced costs with benefits. After all, they were just as much affected by the plan and the cost of the plan as I was. In time, picking plans became a group exercise where we evaluated the plan benefits and costs. Everyone sees the costs, calculates how much each plan will cost them after the company pays half, and understands the benefits of each plan. Although I make the final decision on which plan we go with every year, I seek their feedback and insights.

My first employee, whose husband was in the military, opted out of the new company health insurance plan, as expected. But it turned out that my second employee didn't need it either. It was cheaper for him to get insurance on his wife's company's plan. Only me and my family signed up for the plan.

That was a win for me. I was now an employer who offered health insurance, which made recruiting top talent easier. But at the same time, none of my employees enrolled in the plan, so I saved a bunch of money.

Dental and vision insurance were relatively inexpensive compared to health insurance, so we added those insurance plans shortly thereafter. Like with health insurance, we paid 50 percent of the premium. With those three—health, dental, and vision—and with paid time off, I had most of the major perks covered.

Later, at the request of an employee, we added long-term disability insurance, short-term disability insurance, and life insurance. Like dental and vision insurance, these three new policies combined were inexpensive. But unlike the other policies, I initially decided to pay 100 percent of the premium. Not surprisingly, everyone signed up.

About a year later, while scrutinizing our financials during one of our many cash crunches, the payments for short- and long-term disability and life insurance caught my eye. It was only a few hundred dollars a month, but I wondered if my employees valued those plans. No one ever mentioned how much they appreciated them, and the benefits had never been used by anyone in the company.

The only way I was going to find out if they valued the benefit was to ask. But asking wasn't enough. When something is given to you for free, you may not value it even though you've accepted it. Why would you turn it away if it's free? So I had to see if employees would be willing to pay for part of this benefit the same way they paid for part of health, dental, and vision.

After explaining that I was considering dropping the perk, but wanting to see if employees wanted to keep it, I asked if they'd prefer we drop it or split the cost with them like we did for health, dental, and vision. To my surprise, most wanted the perk and were willing to pay for it. The tribe had spoken!

With the next payroll, we split the difference with employees. There were a few grumblings about them now having to pay 50 percent of the cost for something they used to get for free, but no one dropped the benefit. Had I to do it all over again, I would have initially offered to pay for 50 percent of that perk instead of paying for it all.

Slowly we added more perks. When I noticed that several employees were going to the gym after work, I got with my gym and opened a corporate account. Similar to insurance, we'd have the employees pay part of this perk. We'd pay the joining fee and the monthly fee, but we'd withhold a measly five dollars per paycheck. It obviously wasn't a lot, but I wanted them to have a reminder that they were paying for a perk, so they would not waste it.

Yet, I knew that wouldn't be enough to get people to the gym. I wanted them to be healthy and work out, but I also didn't want to keep paying for a membership that they weren't going to use, even if they did pay for a small portion of it. So I added a clause requesting that they go at least once a week. Another caveat was that if they didn't go for an entire month, then we'd stop paying for the membership. They can keep the membership if they want, but if they weren't using it, then we would stop paying for it.

When I first rolled out the gym perk, practically everyone took advantage of it. That first week, I saw everyone at the gym working out, doing cardio, and a few of the guys playing racquetball. But starting the second week, it was back to normal. They quickly stopped using the perk. I didn't cut them off after a month, even though the employee policies said they should be cut off, but once someone didn't show for two months, I cut them off.

Over time, only a small portion of employees would use the gym membership. To keep administration of the plan simple, it only applied to the line of gyms I attended, so I could easily find out how often my folks worked out. One problem was that only people who worked out of the main office could use the perk. That means remote workers couldn't take advantage of that perk. I thought about opening that perk up to any gym anywhere, but then I'd open myself up to variable, and potentially costly, monthly gym fees, and I'd have no way of knowing if the perk was being used.

Perhaps I should have treated the gym membership perk just like any other, with the company paying half. But it doesn't matter now because we've since canceled this perk due to low participation. In the end, no one cared much about it.

Even with health insurance, paid time off, and a stable of other minor perks in place, one perk eluded me for many years. That was a retirement plan.

Every job I'd had since graduating college had come with a retirement plan. It was another big perk that I felt we needed to offer. Without it, we were an employer with an inferior set of benefits to offer employees and potential employees. We felt that we had to offer a retirement plan to finally become a legitimate employer.

Connecting with a local financial advisor, we asked about setting up a 401(k) plan. We were advised that a 401(k) plan would be quite expensive for a small company, and 401(k)s were best suited for companies with at least fifty employees. What was best for us was a SIMPLE IRA.

Both 401(k)s and SIMPLE IRAs allow employees to put away a portion of their pre-tax dollars into a retirement account, and the employer can match a certain percentage. SIMPLE IRAs allowed us to match 100 percent of the employee's first 3 percent of their salary, which is what we did.

It was quite painless for us to open the retirement plan. The financial advisor did the heavy lifting and met with each employee to explain all their options and work with them to invest their savings into various mutual funds. At the company level, though, it did add the extra expense of matching our employees' contributions. Everyone participated, so our payroll cost effectively increased 3 percent.

With the retirement plan in place, we had finally put all the pieces into place to take care of our employees. Like with other aspects of entrepreneurship, when it came to offering benefits, I felt it was better to start, even if in an imperfect way, than to wait to create a mega-comprehensive plan. We got the basics into place and made them better over time. That turned out to be a much better solution than not hiring anyone until I had a full and expensive arsenal of benefits to offer the first person.

Incremental improvement, as with most areas of business, worked out well for offering employee benefits. When you're preparing to hire your first employee, I recommend you iterate your employee benefits as well.

Before you start interviewing people, decide on which benefits you want to provide. Prospective employees will likely ask about benefits during the interview process, and it's best to have a clear understanding of what you want to offer. It's also a good idea to have at least a rough understanding of how much each benefit will cost you.

But if you're not sure which possible benefits they value, then work with your first employees to come up with a benefits package that works for you and for them. Like I did, you can adjust by adding or removing benefits over time.

→ Employee review processes

Going through an early growth phase, we quickly grew from a one-man shop to having three or four full-time employees and one part-time employee. Things were humming along in the human resources department just fine for quite some time.

That is, until one of my guys who had been with me for a little over a year asked me if I would give him a review. He said he'd like to get my feedback on how he'd performed the previous year and wanted to know what he could do to add more value to the company.

I was surprised that an employee actually wanted a review. As a former employee myself, I dreaded the process of the annual review. It was a bit of a shock to me that others, people who now worked for me, sought out that kind of feedback.

I found out later that in addition to the review, he also wanted a raise. Ha! And here I was thinking he just wanted to know how he could do better! Regardless of his motivation for requesting it, I had enough employees where I could no longer just hope no one asked for a raise. But before handing out raises, a review was in order. It was time for me to create a review and raise process.

I dreaded creating a process for reviews and raises. I feared putting a process like that into place because I was, and still am, firmly anti-bureaucratic. Ever since I graduated from college and started my career, I'd been subjected to the same process for employee reviews.

Once a year, the whole company would be completely distracted with reviews for about a month. The month-long distraction would kick off with our human resources (HR) folks briefing everyone on the review process.

Reviews consisted of several questions that both the employee and the supervisor would have to answer or comment on. You know ... how well the employee performed, what their strengths and weaknesses were, something they did well last year, and areas of improvement. As the employee being reviewed, I would fill out my answers to those questions, my manager would provide responses to my answers, and then we'd compare my responses to my supervisor's responses.

What I quickly realized was that the employee always writes up all the good things they've done for the last year while glossing over the not-so-good things. The supervisor would do basically the opposite. They'd focus on the negatives more than the positives, acknowledge the good performance but without giving too much credit.

It was a dance the employee and supervisor did every year, where the employee wanted to be seen as a top contributor to the company, and the supervisor basically knocked their direct report down to earth while still propping them up just enough to make it look like they were a good supervisor.

On my first review as an employee out of college, and naive to the game, I listed a few of my weaknesses in my review. It was an honest assessment of where I was just one year out of college. My supervisor, who was, frankly, more of a friend than a supervisor, cautioned me to not include negative comments about myself in reviews.

He explained how the review process is a game corporations play, and that as the employee, my objective was to only include my accomplishments and strengths in the review. He told me to never list a weakness or mention something I had screwed up. Basically, as the employee, I needed to create the narrative that I walked on water.

Having been schooled by my corporate mentor, I played the game from then on. Later, as a supervisor, I continued to play the game, pointing out the weaknesses and mess-ups my folks had done during the past year. But every time I participated in this game, I felt dirty. Something just didn't seem right about the whole employee review process.

Worse, at my last job, supervisors had to grade each employee by giving them a 1–5 rating on different questions. The HR briefing to supervisors made it abundantly clear that they expected very few 1s and very few 5s to be issued. Doing so would require substantial evidence to support your rating.

If you gave someone a shoulder rating of a 2 or a 4, then you had to leave a brief comment to explain why they deserved that rating. But if you gave a 3, no comment was necessary. A 3 on a 1–5 scale just flew right on by … no comment or documentation necessary.

Guess what the average rating was across the company? It was slightly higher than a 3. Now why would that be?

If you make it hard to provide honest feedback and doing so will require a lot of extra work, people will simply take the path of least resistance. Supervisors are no different. Since the average rating was a little over a 3, it showed that they were willing to do just a tad bit of extra work by doling out a 4 every once in a while.

To summarize my prior experience with reviews, they weren't great. They were games played by employees and supervisors, and I hated playing the game. Once I had my own company, I was determined to stop playing those kinds of stupid games.

What I wanted out of a review process was the ability to provide real feedback and have an honest discussion. I also didn't want to wait until just one day of the year. The review process needed a more frequent feedback loop between supervisors and employees.

Knowing generally what I wanted, but unsure of exactly how it should be structured, I started researching different ways that modern companies handle their review and raise processes. A model that resonated with me was that of Silicon Valley tech startups. Although they could afford to lavish their employees with ridiculous perks, and I could not, I plucked some of the good parts out of what I discovered and cobbled together my own review process.

→ One-on-one meetings

First, I wanted to ensure that discussions were held regularly between employee and supervisor. That required dedicated, on-the-calendar time between the two parties. At that point, I was the only supervisor in the company, so I'd schedule a lunch meeting between me and every employee once every two months. I named these one-on-one meetings "1-1" for short.

The company would pay for lunch, we'd talk about how things were going, and I'd provide feedback on any concerns I had. It was a time for us to air any grievances from either side and conclude with what the next two months would entail before we got together again.

Later, as some of my employees had their own direct reports, they'd meet over lunch. This worked okay at first, but it didn't seem to have the same impact for other supervisors as it did for me. When I'd ask about how the lunch went, about half the time it turned out they just chatted over a free lunch and never got around to talking about how the employee was performing.

I was surprised when I realized that many times most supervisors and direct reports would even skip their 1-1. Wanting to ensure that employees got supervisor facetime like I wanted them to, we started to track each 1-1 to ensure that it was held.

Clearly, they weren't seeing value in the process I had set up. That was a disappointment, but I didn't know how to improve the process. I was already paying them to have a free lunch on me. What more was needed to get them to talk?

Then I learned the concept of holding weekly 1-1s during a learning session hosted by the Entrepreneurs' Organization. The trainer extolled the virtues of holding a weekly meeting or phone call between each supervisor/direct report. But he also told us to keep them short, preferably no more than fifteen minutes each. Although to me it seemed like overkill and potentially a giant waste of time to meet with each direct report weekly, I decided to give it a shot. It turned out to be great advice!

We continue holding weekly 1-1s between each supervisor and employee. I currently hold five 1-1s with each of my direct reports every Wednesday morning. I allocate half an hour to each in case we go over, although it's perfectly fine if we wrap up in ten minutes or if we use the entire thirty minutes. Those five meetings happen one after the other, so my entire morning is booked.

Seems like a lot, but it's time well-invested. I consider these to be the most important set of meetings I have all week.

→ Kudos

Our kudos system was detailed earlier in *Million Dollar Journey*. One reason I instituted it was so I could find out about the good things people were doing in the company. Oftentimes, even supervisors aren't aware of all of their direct reports' contributions. Many good things employees do are never noticed at a higher level, and that's a shame.

If Steve takes twenty minutes to help Samantha out with a problem she's struggling with, that collaboration is a good thing. But Steve's boss will likely never hear about it.

With kudos in place, and an incentive program tied to it for giving and receiving kudos, that information sees the light of day. When Samantha thanks Steve by giving him kudos, Steve's supervisor will see that.

That kind of feedback, which was made intentionally public to the whole company, is great input into the 1-1 meetings between supervisors and direct reports. Those kudos can, and should, be used to directly influence more formal reviews as well.

→ Annual reviews

Although I hated the annual review process I'd been subjected to in the past, I knew I needed an annual review process for the company. But the big difference between what my past employers did and the process I would create would be that there should be no surprises, on either side, at the annual review.

After all, supervisors and direct reports were having dedicated time once a week to discuss these kinds of things. Anything of concern, anything that could end up in the annual review, would certainly have already been discussed once or more during these 1-1 meetings. If they hadn't, or if someone came out of an annual meeting surprised, then the supervisor wasn't doing a good job with their 1-1 meetings, or with supervising.

What I definitely didn't want was the same old process where the employee said how amazing they've been, but conveniently forgot about all of their oopsies, and the supervisor reminded them of all the screw-ups they'd made along the way. Since the annual review would be mostly a recap of previous conversations, the supervisor should simply document those conversations and present it to their direct report. Each time we've done that, the response has basically been, "Yah, I agree with that." We also provide a space for the employee to provide their own comments for any reason.

Rolling out the stack of processes for reviews—1-1s, kudos, and annual reviews—went practically flawlessly. Besides changing the 1-1s from a free lunch every other month to weekly fifteen-minute meetings, everything else has remained as originally laid out.

→ Raises

Raises are a funny thing. Employees want the biggest raise possible, but companies generally want them to be as low as possible. They're yet another point of contention in the human resources realm. But before talking about a raise, you have to conduct a review to see how the employee is doing.

The annual review is used as input into a discussion between me and each supervisor about how much of a raise we should give an employee. In the beginning, we didn't have a great way to deal with raises. I had yet to create the process, which meant that I tried all sorts of options with varying degrees of success.

Frankly, it's still a work in process. But originally, we would negotiate each raise with each person. That resulted in some people getting substantially more than others due to their negotiating skill, which arguably may have resulted in their raise being disproportionate to their actual contribution.

The point of a raise is to provide an annual salary adjustment. It is not meant, per se, to compensate someone for doing a bigger, more valuable job, than they are supposed to be doing. In those circumstances, you should be considering a promotion, not just a raise. I'll circle back to promotions in the next section.

Simply doing your job as you said you would does not entitle you to getting a big, fat raise. After all, you said you'd do it for a certain amount, then you did it. You don't get a big raise for doing what was expected of you.

A raise, in my opinion, should be a moderate, yet noticeable, annual increase if the person is doing everything expected of them. Granted, some may be contributing much less or much more than others, and that should be reflected in the amount of each person's raise. But still, the raise should be a modest bump in pay.

That's true for most companies, but I've adopted a stance that it's not okay to contribute "much less" than expected. In those circumstances, we shouldn't even be talking about a raise; we should be talking about a performance improvement plan or disciplinary action.

If an employee is not doing well, they shouldn't get a raise. Thanks to our weekly 1-1s and a formal disciplinary process, the fact that they are underperforming should come as no surprise to the employee.

Since we have a baseline criteria that raises are only for those doing well, and everyone else will be going down the route of disciplinary action and a performance improvement plan, we've recently adopted a policy of largely standardizing our raise amounts. We've also split the raise into two components—a salary adjustment and a bonus.

Let's say someone is doing everything you expect of them, and you've established that their performance warrants a 6 percent raise. One option is to simply raise their salary by 6 percent. The downside for the company is that the raise next year will be on top of the raise from this year. In other words, raises compound over time.

What we decided to do instead is break up the increase into a salary increase and a bonus. So instead of getting a 6 percent raise, they actually get a 4 percent salary increase and a 2 percent bonus. That bonus would be paid out immediately (the next paycheck issued), and the salary increase would kick in then too.

So the employee gets a one-time cash bonus of 2 percent of their current salary and does not need to wait for the whole year to receive it little by little in each paycheck. That addresses the downside for the employee. On the employer side, they've only increased their salary baseline by 4 percent instead of 6 percent, removing some of the compounding effect.

Raises should be put in writing, ideally by updating or amending the employment agreement you have with each employee, every time they get a raise. No matter what, somehow put it in writing. You should identify when the raise takes effect, and the amount of the salary adjustment and bonus. That written record should then go into the employee's personnel file.

→ **Promotions**

A job promotion should only be given when you've clearly defined the new responsibilities and duties that the person will take on.

In the past, I've made the mistake of giving people "promotions" simply by giving them a bigger title in order to make Array Digital look bigger than we were at the time. You know the trick … when a company has, say, three people, and everyone is a CEO, VP, or Chief Something Or Other, even though they're all really junior-level folks.

It sure looks good at a company level when you tell someone you'll have your VP of Product Development contact them. But when your VP turns out to be more junior than the client they're calling, it doesn't look so good. It may help with initial perceptions, but it can make you look foolish later.

Another problem with promoting by title without thinking it through is that titles mean something. Although you personally may no longer care about titles, you're also the entrepreneur in charge of your company. You've already declared yourself king. Titles don't mean much to you anymore, but they certainly mean something to the people who work for you.

If you bump someone from designer to senior designer in order to make your proposals look more appealing, then guess what? At some point, whether they're capable or not, they'll start to believe that they should be paid like a senior designer! If they can't perform at that level, then you've just set yourself up for a very awkward future conversation.

I once hired a mid-level person but at the last minute, decided to bestow a director title upon them. I wanted their title to be impressive to the outside world. Although the title was impressive, the employee wasn't up to the expectation. I piled on more responsibilities than they could handle, and they ended up crashing and burning. Providing a lofty title set them up for failure, and that was my fault.

I had done the same thing when we hired Jake to be our digital marketing "guy." His job was to provide digital marketing after we delivered a website to our clients. When we hired him, he was somewhere between advanced junior-level and early mid-level in his career. But we knew that if he was going in front of clients talking about digital marketing, we'd have to give him a title that puffed him up a bit. Although he had little management experience at the time, we settled on the title digital marketing manager.

We all acknowledged that was a bigger title than he deserved at the time, and we joked about it often. But over time, he grew into the title and later performed well at it. So much so that after a few years, I realized we needed to groom him into a bigger position. One that we lacked and badly needed—a creative director.

Upon bringing this up to him at one of our weekly 1-1s, Jake latched onto the idea. He said he was ready, but I countered that he wasn't. He needed to learn a lot more about the industry and the history of marketing and advertising, and he needed to grow into the position. I didn't want to give him that title before he was ready because it could not only set him up for failure, it could also hurt his reputation and career. I didn't want him to become the laughingstock of the marketing community if they realized it was a lofty title that he didn't deserve. So I made him wait.

Over the course of more than a year, we'd talk about the possible promotion. I told him that I frankly didn't know exactly what I expected out of a creative director and asked him to research the job responsibilities. He did, and I did too, but he's the one who drafted the job requirements. But still, he wasn't quite ready.

More time passed, and I watched as he began taking more ownership of the creative process and output. He was slowly starting to operate in the capacity of a creative director, a position we still did not have in the company. Along the way, we talked about it every two or three weeks during our weekly 1-1s and discussed how he had recently demonstrated the ability to be a creative director and where he still came up a bit short.

Time went on, but I still didn't think he was ready. After about a year and a half of discussion, and coming up on his annual review, I recognized the effort he'd put in. He'd been reading, studying, and getting better about being assertive with his team. He'd gotten heavily involved with the local professional organization for marketers. He was beginning to control the creative process, output, and team. He was ready.

At his review, we discussed all the things we had covered in the weekly 1-1s since his last review. When it came time to talk about his performance and a possible promotion, no one was surprised. It was clear he was ready. He once again pitched the promotion, and this time I agreed.

I announced to the team not only his promotion, but discussed the one-and-a-half-year process we went through to get him ready. I explained how he was now ready and how his responsibilities were shifting accordingly.

That was one of the better promotions I've given. He was not only eager but willing to put in the work to get himself ready. It was a well-deserved promotion, and even Jake appreciates that it was not a promotion in title only. He had to earn it. I hope future promotions go as smoothly as that one did.

The big lesson I've learned about promotions is to not hand them out willy-nilly. If you do, they will be meaningless.

Be sure you understand the new responsibilities that come along with the promotion. If you're not 100 percent sure you understand, then hold back on making the promotion. Of course, also be 100 percent sure your employee understands the new expectations. If you're not clear, or they're not clear, it could mean big trouble ahead for you both and for your company. Also, be sure the position they're being promoted into is one that the company needs. Never create a new position just to placate an employee's ambitions.

Titles matter, and you control those titles. Take that responsibility seriously.

Chapter takeaways

1. Core values are beliefs that you, as the founder, should put into writing and build into every aspect of working at your company. It's okay to add, edit, or even remove core values over time as you learn more about how you want your company to evolve.
2. Most employees expect not only pay, but also benefits. Consider the cost of each benefit before you offer it to employees. Like most areas of business, it's perfectly acceptable to iterate the benefits you offer and change them over time as your company grows.
3. Provide continual feedback to employees on their performance. Consider holding short weekly one-on-one meetings between supervisors and their direct reports.
4. Create a method for employees to publicly recognize each other's contributions. This will help create a sense of team and also help supervisors discover good things their employees are doing.
5. When creating your annual review process, create one that encourages open and honest feedback. No one should be surprised in an annual review.
6. Pay raises should be moderate adjustments in pay.
7. Larger raises should come with more responsibilities and be considered a promotion, but only if you need that position filled.

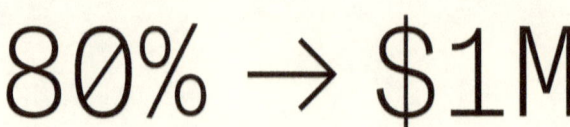

→ 12

Goal-setting

Goals come in many forms. Personal, professional, short-term, long-term, and even New Year's resolutions.

I like the analogy of setting goals and driving a car. If you don't set a goal, it's like getting in your car and driving. You'll be going somewhere, but if you don't know the destination, how do you know you're even driving in the right direction?

You may be asking yourself, *Should we set goals early in our journey?*

Or, *Why wasn't goal-setting one of the first chapters in Million Dollar Journey?*

Great questions—here's why.

→ When to set your business goals

Most business books tell you to set your goals first before doing anything else. They say you should write a business plan. The bigger the better. You should anticipate every future opportunity, obstacle, and risk. And they say you should plot your plan for the next twenty years.

But in my experience, that's not a great way to start a business. When you don't know what you're doing, and you don't know where you're going yet, then creating a thick business plan complete with projections and assumptions doesn't help you much. I've tried it before and promptly ignored the business plan once I got going, because it was garbage. You can't predict the future when the future is uncertain.

You must validate what you're doing first before you set goals beyond that. In the beginning, you need to think one or two steps ahead of your current situation. The important idea at this stage is simply to get going. The more time you spend writing a business plan, the more time you're not starting your business. Start your business, figure out your business as you run it, and once you have confidence in what you're doing, you can set your goals.

That applies to life too.

→ Don't lie to yourself

How many times have you set a goal, but you didn't mean it? How many times did you tell someone what your goal was, but you smirked or laughed when you said it?

New Year's resolutions are goals just like any others. With New Year's resolutions, in particular, many of us lie to ourselves the moment the words escape our mouths. For some reason, our society accepts that most people don't intend to keep their New Year's resolutions.

If your goal is to get in shape, then you'll go to the gym a couple of times in January. But like in years past, you'll likely falter and stop going by Valentine's Day. I witness that cycle firsthand every year in my gym, with an influx of new members in January who mysteriously vanish by the spring.

Another common resolution is to eat better. Sure, you'll eat better for a few days. But a month into the new year, and you'll be back to pizza, wings, and beers on Friday nights. You know it's true!

It's a shame, really. Why even go through the charade of setting a New Year's resolution, or any goal, if you don't mean it? Either say it and mean it, or don't say it at all.

I've discovered a handful of ways that I've been able to reach my goals, personally and professionally, even after the novelty of goal-setting has worn off. The principles that follow have helped me achieve my goals and have accelerated my entrepreneurial journey.

The only reason I finished *Million Dollar Journey* was because I set a New Year's resolution and respected the principles that follow. Without these principles, I would have walked away from a half-written book a long time ago.

These principles can help you set and achieve goals for your business and for yourself.

→ Set specific goals

Acronyms abound in the business world that describe how to set goals. SMART is one such acronym that people often employ.

SMART stands for specific, measurable, achievable, relevant, and time-based. I agree with most of these components, but not all of them. As an example, when I decided one year that I was going to run more, I realized I needed to be more specific. So I set a goal to run 1,000 miles by the end of the year.

The goal was specific—I would run 1,000 miles. It was measurable—I could record how far I ran each time and add the miles up. It was time-based—it had to be finished by the end of the year.

But I nailed only three of the five components in SMART. Why not the other two? Was it Achievable? Maybe. Maybe not.

I had never run 1,000 miles in a year. Shoot, I didn't even know how many miles I'd run in any prior year because I had never tracked my mileage like that. I had no baseline to determine if my goal was achievable.

But I was determined. I knew I could run three miles at a time and do that several days in a row. I also knew that if I ran three miles every day, and with a year having 365 days, I could run up to 1,095 miles if I never missed a day. That would give me a ninety-five-mile buffer for the days that I was sick, hurt, or just couldn't find the time or motivation to run. So I was confident I could run 1,000 miles, but I didn't know if the goal was actually achievable.

Was it relevant? Not exactly. I hadn't set a running goal before and wasn't even running all that much prior to setting the goal. The reason I picked it was for a personal challenge. To prove to myself that I can achieve whatever I set my mind to.

Another resolution I made that year was to come to a complete stop at stop signs and stop lights. The rolling stops were getting out of hand! That wasn't relevant to anything except, once again, a personal challenge. Relevance, for my own New Year's resolutions at least, turns out to not be that relevant.

To be completely transparent, I had to Google what SMART goals stood for. It's a great rule of thumb for goal-setting, but in the end, you simply need to have the conviction that you will set out to do what you tell yourself you're going to do. Don't lie to yourself, and be clear on what your goal is.

Be specific, then simply do it. You either want to achieve your goal, or you don't. It's that simple.

→ Track your progress

Once I decided to run 1,000 miles in a year, guess what I started doing next? I went for a run! After running a few times, I realized that I needed to write down each time I ran. I wanted to make sure I ran 1,000 miles, so I needed to log each run.

Tracking my progress seemed pretty obvious to me, but this is an important step that many people skip. If you don't track how you're doing against your goals, then you're simply guessing. Guessing may get you close, but then again, you have no idea.

I had already established that I needed to maintain a pace of three miles per day on average to safely reach my goal of 1,000 miles by the end of the year. So as long as I kept close to that pace, I'd be in good shape to achieve the goal by the end of the year.

Tracking my mileage in a spreadsheet allowed me to easily add up how far I'd run for the year. I also created a formula to determine how many miles I should have run based on the current day of the year. With that, I could compare how many miles I'd run so far that year against how many miles I had to run by that date in order to finish by the end of the year. Suddenly, I could determine quickly if I was on pace or not to reach my goal.

Tracking my progress led to accountability. Knowing if I was ahead of or behind pace was key for me. Any time I got behind, it was a motivating factor to run another half mile here or there to catch up.

Whatever your goal, personal or professional, if it's a measurable and time-sensitive goal, then you can track your progress over time. Track your progress in a spreadsheet or other system, and determine if you are on pace to hit your goal or not. If you find that you're not on pace, you'll know exactly what you need to do to get back on track.

→ Public accountability

Key performance indicators (KPIs) are a way that businesses track how they're doing. As a business founder, you'll likely have a handful of important KPIs that you want to track over time.

At Array Digital, we set goals, KPIs, for the quarter. Progress toward achieving each KPI is tracked and reported weekly. Each KPI has an owner—the person responsible for achieving the goal. The owner of the KPI has to personally report their progress at our company meeting. Having the KPI owner brief everyone else on their progress is a form of public accountability.

You can also apply this principle to your personal goals.

Once I knew how far I needed to have run by the current date and how far I had actually run, I had enough data to report to others on how I was doing. Every week, I reported publicly, on Twitter, of how I was doing against my running goal.

I decided to publicly self-report for three reasons:

First, I was confident enough in myself that I was sure I'd hit the goal.

Second, I wanted to set an example for other entrepreneurs that big goals are achievable. Although you can lie to yourself when you set your goals, you're unlikely to highlight the lie to the world by admitting that you failed to reach your goals. I wasn't about to lie about my goals to everyone who was watching me. I said I'd run 1,000 miles, and I was going to figure out a way to do just that.

Third, I knew that holding myself publicly accountable would motivate me to continue. And it did. On many mornings, I just wanted to sleep in. My calves were sore for the first six months of the year. Walking hurt, and running hurt even worse. I had plenty of reasons to quit. But I knew I had to self-report every Monday, and I wasn't going to report that I was a quitter. Knowing that Monday was public accountability day kept me going when I may have otherwise quit.

→ Learning curves

Taking on new skills is tough. You're no good at it at first, but you get better over time.

I recently took my daughter out to drive a stick shift car for the first time. At first, she stalled five times in a row. But after an hour of learning, she was driving us all over town. She got better with time.

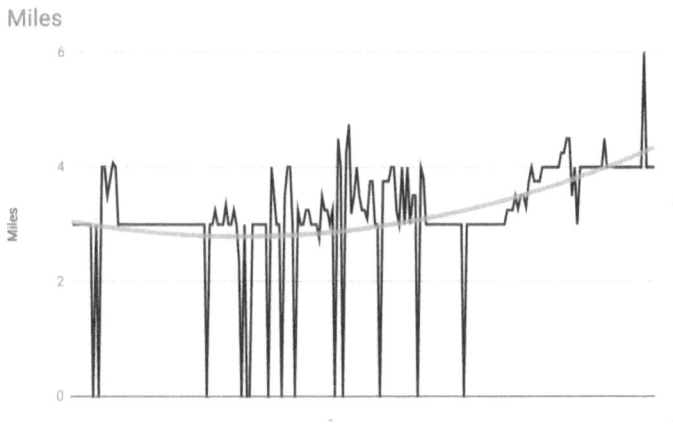

Like learning to drive, learning curves apply to goals. The chart shows the number of miles I ran every day when I was trying to run those 1,000 miles in a year. The jagged line shows the number of miles I ran each day, and the curve is the trend.

Notice that after missing two days early on, I hit a streak for the first two or three months of the year. But then I started to miss more days in the second quarter. The novelty of consistently running had worn off, and my calves were still sore. It wasn't fun anymore. The trendline dipped down around the second quarter of the year as the grind continued. I started to take more days off from running.

In the middle of June, my calves suddenly loosened up. Running three miles was much easier than before, and I began to increase my mileage, just a bit at first to 3.25 miles each time, then to 3.5 miles. By the fourth quarter of the year, my new daily run was four miles long. On the weekends, I'd even go six to eight miles. As my body got used to running, I had overcome the learning curve.

You may experience the same curve when pursuing your goals. Initially you'll be fired up. But soon the reality will set in, and you'll hit an initial bump in the road. If you convince yourself to keep going, you'll have a good streak, but at some point, the novelty will wear off. You can either quit at that point, or dig deeper to find enough discipline to complete your goal.

Setting goals is easy. Finishing them takes determination. Just don't give up.

→ Small changes over time

Right around the time my calves finally loosened up, I had an epiphany. In order to get back on pace, I had to run 3.25 miles every day for a couple of weeks. At about halfway through the year, I realized that if I had always run that extra quarter mile, I would have been forty miles closer to my goal.

It was shocking to discover that I could have gained such an advantage by simply running another quarter mile, or extra two-and-a-half minutes, each day. After already running for twenty-five minutes or so each time, an extra two-and-a-half minutes would have been barely noticeable. It just goes to show that if you make a small change, and sustain that change over time, the impact can be huge.

> **Erik J. Olson**
> @iamerikjolson
>
> Can't believe I just figured out that if I had run an extra 1/4 mile per day, I'd be 40 miles closer to my 1k mile goal for 2019.
>
> Just goes to show, how little things over time will add up.
>
> Started running that extra bit yesterday!
>
> 10:30 AM · Jun 21, 2019

This is the magic behind long-term goal-setting. Think long term, then set shorter-term goals that get you closer to your long-term goals.

Be specific, measure how you're doing, and report on your progress. These principles apply to your personal goals as well as to your professional goals. Above all else, keep pushing forward.

Just like with any major endeavor, the way to reach your first $1 million in revenue is to start with a goal. But unlike others who give up on their goals, you can follow the goal-setting principles we just went over to ensure you achieve them.

→ Short-term versus long-term goals

When setting goals, select a time horizon that you're aiming for. Do you want to accomplish the goal in three months, a year, or in ten years? The shorter the time horizon, the easier it is to concretely select a goal. Projecting further into the future is more difficult because it's hard to fathom the compounding effect of goal-setting.

People often overestimate what they'll accomplish in one year, but underestimate what they can accomplish in ten years.

In the last few years, I went through the exercise of setting short-term and long-term goals for Array Digital. Setting a short-term goal for the next year was relatively easy. I looked back at how we'd grown in the past year or two, projected that growth into the future by one year, and stretched it a bit.

Using round numbers as an example, let's say we did $500K in revenue two years ago and $1M in revenue last year. That's growing by

$500K per year. Certainly, we could continue that trend this year, right? So a goal of $1.5M would be achievable if nothing else changed.

But what about a ten-year revenue goal? Should we assume that we could continue to grow another $500K each year? That'd put us at about $5M in ten years.

Remember that people underestimate what they can accomplish in ten years. What if we instead estimated aggressively? Instead of projecting a $500K increase every year, why not project a continued growth rate of 100 percent every year, just like last year? If so, we'd grow into a $500M company in just ten years. Sounds ridiculous, right? Is that achievable? What would it take to continue to grow at 100 percent for ten years straight?

Well, we'd need to hire a sales force, get into bigger markets, and get bigger clients.

Now let's take this scenario and apply it to your business, but with different numbers. Let's start with the first task—creating a sales force. What will that take? If you don't have a salesperson right now, start there, and hire your first salesperson.

If you did that this year, could you hire a second salesperson next year, and two more the year after, and four more the year after that? Probably, but it'd require better cash flow and more efficient processes. Maybe you should fix your cash flow or process issues at the same time.

See how one huge goal is starting to be broken down into smaller goals? To grow 100 percent for ten years straight will require a series of other goals.

Suddenly you're exploring what it would take to achieve what at first seemed like an outrageous goal. When you break it down into small, manageable steps, it doesn't seem quite so inconceivable. I'm not saying that just because you set a huge goal, you'll achieve it. But if you don't set a huge goal, you'll never explore whether it's really possible.

Chapter takeaways

1. If you set goals for your entrepreneurial journey too early, then you may be guessing. Start on the journey, figure out your business model, then set goals based on what you've learned so far.
2. When you set a goal, be honest with yourself. If you don't intend to achieve a goal, don't say you will. Never lie to yourself. If you say you'll do it, then do it.
3. When setting goals, be specific and set measurable goals. Track your progress daily in a spreadsheet, and hold yourself publicly accountable.
4. Like most new areas of life, you'll experience a learning curve as you work toward achieving your goals.
5. Small improvements, performed consistently over time, will yield large results.
6. Setting long-term goals is typically harder than setting short-term goals. But once you set a long-term goal, work backward by setting multiple short-term goals along the way.

MILLION DOLLAR JOURNEY

→ 13

Pivoting

As you continue to grow your business, you'll start to better understand the advantages and the pitfalls of the business you're in. If you're like me, then you'll start, or have already started, a business based on the expertise you've acquired up to that point. But just because you're doing something you're good at doesn't mean it's the best business for you to be in.

When I went into business for myself, I was a software developer, so that's the kind of business I started. I was able to get the company up and running, but it always struggled to scale.

First, it was difficult to explain the industry niche I was in. No matter how I explained to people that I built sophisticated data-driven web applications, people unfamiliar with the niche always thought I was either an IT guy or a website guy. Neither of those oversimplifications were quite right. Since it wasn't clear to most people what I did, how could I expect them to give me referrals? Turns out, they couldn't. Leads were hard to come by.

Second, it was near impossible to identify who needed my services. Some of our clients were startups, some were Fortune 500s. Most were somewhere in between. There were no external attributes that I could use to determine if any given person or business may need our services. In a room of one hundred people, I had no clue whatsoever as to whether someone needed us or not. I'd have to talk to every person in the room and hope they expressed interest in my service after they learned what I did.

Add to that the rapid changes in the software development world. The quality of offshore development had been steadily improving for years, and they were much less expensive than what I was charging. The competitive advantages I had—being an American, working the same hours as my clients, and understanding their idioms and inflexions—was once enough to convince people to pay more for me. But with offshoring noticeably improving and being less expensive, it became harder for me to overcome those objections.

On one project, we had been paired with an offshore development company out of Costa Rica. They were just one time zone behind us, so they worked the same hours as our clients for all practical purposes. They used the same tools as we did, and unlike deliverables from other offshore companies we'd inherited over the years, their work was high quality. They even joked around with us and our mutual client. They were half the price as us and just as good. I was losing my competitive advantage.

→ In search of a partner

More frequently than before, clients who hired me to build a sophisticated, data-driven application also needed a marketing website. Having built many applications that didn't succeed in the past, I knew that a product needed a marketing website to explain what that product was and why a customer should try it.

I'd learned that lesson early on with Measured Mile and saw it play out over and over again with my clients. Building a custom web application or a mobile app wasn't good enough. A marketing website was needed to provide an overview of the product and to persuade people to try it.

Having turned away marketing work in the past, but seeing the shift in my niche occurring before my eyes, I decided we would try our hand at also building marketing websites for our clients. We were developers, after all, so how hard could it be?

Well, it was harder than I expected. As developers, we could build anything, and it would work great, but it probably wouldn't look great. We weren't designers, and at the time, we didn't understand the art of persuasion or of sales copywriting. After trying to build a couple of marketing websites, I decided that I needed to find a web designer who I could partner with.

That's when I bumped into Kevin Daisey at a learning event. He and his company only built marketing websites. After chatting for a bit, and me explaining that I needed a web design company to build marketing websites for my clients, he mentioned that he had a similar issue. But for him, it was just the opposite. He could design something to look great, but could only provide the functionality that came out of the frameworks he used. When a client wanted something else, something custom, his options to satisfy his clients were limited.

Knowing we could help each other, we said that we'd refer each other when there were opportunities. He then mentioned that he had a prospect who not only needed a marketing website, but also needed a more sophisticated database application. He said he'd connect the dots and set up a meeting with the prospect.

The prospect already knew Kevin, but now it was time for him to meet me. A meeting was set up with Kevin's prospect at my office. The prospect was eager to begin and well-funded, and signed contracts with both Kevin and me within a week of that first meeting.

The concept was that Kevin's team and my team would work closely to design and build a marketing website and a custom application for the client. We had worked with other design companies in the past, but never quite that closely or on a project that large.

The project lasted for months, and our teams got to know one another. We often collaborated online, occasionally worked at each other's offices, and respected the work that the other group was doing. Seeing how well the teams worked together and how much fun this project was turning out to be, it was apparent that working together was a winning combination. This revelation led to many conversations between Kevin and me about the struggles each of us faced in our companies.

Some of my clients who hired me to build sophisticated, data-intensive applications also needed marketing websites, which I didn't do. Some of his clients who hired him to build marketing websites also need sophisticated data-intensive applications.

Turns out our combined clients didn't quite understand the differences between what each of us did because they were asking each of us for stuff we did not actually do. Clients would want to give us the whole project, even if the parts we couldn't do in-house, but we each needed to find someone else to do part of the projects. That led to me having work he could do, and him having work I could do.

Through these conversations, we also learned that we each felt stuck at our current market position. I had grown well over the past few years but wasn't confident I'd continue to grow. It was simply too difficult for me to identify and find clients. I knew I would never be able to hire a salesperson to do what I did. That meant that the company would only grow as big as the network I was cultivating. In other words, it would always be limited by my personal reach.

On the contrary, Kevin got plenty of leads. Using SEO and the network he'd built up over the years, his phone would ring off the hook. But many of his prospects were people who wanted to start a business, but had little money for a website. That meant their two or three designers had to build a lot of marketing websites, upward of fifty a year, in order to bring in enough revenue.

Kevin got lots of leads but was stuck doing lower-margin work. I got fewer leads, but when they landed, they were high margin. He wanted higher margins, and I wanted more leads. We each needed what the other had.

→ The merger

Over a beer, I offhandedly commented that we'd kill it if we merged into one company. By that point, our teams had worked on a couple of common projects over the past several months. They knew and liked each other. Kevin and I also worked well together. Turns out, Kevin had been thinking the same thing. We each had what the other wanted, and combined we thought we would have what we would need to make it big.

Casual talk of merging continued for months. Although we both liked the idea, merging would be a major change for both of us, and we proceeded cautiously. Neither of us had ever done anything like this before, so we both asked other entrepreneurs how a merger worked and whether they thought it was a good idea.

We didn't rush into anything. Synergies on that first project led us to jointly pursue other work. He had another prospect who needed a large project built, and it had to be well-designed from a user-experience perspective. It was a good fit for our combined teams, although it would be one of the bigger projects either of us had taken on.

The project would be a stretch for us, but we had all of the talents we needed to pull it off. We pitched the company as a joint effort—two separate companies going after one project. If we were selected, then the client would contract with each of us independently, and we'd work on the project as a collaborative team. That was the plan.

Kevin and I agreed that if we won that project, it was a sign that we had found a business model that worked. Winning the project, one that was bigger than either of us could do on our own, would signal that we needed to merge to get more work like that. We decided that if we won the project, we would definitely merge.

But then the bad news came. We didn't win the project. We were disappointed. The idea of merging suddenly took a backseat.

Wanting to understand why we didn't win the project, we requested a debriefing call with the prospect. During that call they explained to us that one of the main reasons they didn't select us was because they preferred to work with one company instead of two. The company they selected for the project had all the skills in-house, under one roof, to pull off the project.

With that explanation, we realized we would continue to lose bigger projects if we remained small and independent. So although our plan going into the bid was to merge if we won, the actualization that we had lost since we were separate, ironically pushed us to the same conclusion.

We had to merge if we wanted to grow. We wanted bigger projects with bigger clients, and we would never get those, or achieve the goals of scaling our businesses, unless we shook things up.

My first year in business, I made $85K. That was amazing considering I was part time for eight months that year and full time only the last four months. The next year, I pulled in $225K, then $800K the year after that. By the end of 2016, top-line revenue was $900K. I was starting to plateau and getting to that point had drained me. Given how hard it was to find new clients, I had little faith that I'd continue to grow.

A merger would introduce another person who could help organize and run the company. After seven years, Kevin had built his business up to $300K in 2016, but at the burden of having to build over fifty new websites every year. That's a lot of work for not much in return. But work was plentiful and easy for him to find.

Where he experienced steady but slow growth with a lot of volume and low profits, I was just the opposite. We worked with a few clients at a time and generated high profits from each, but sourcing future work was a challenge. Many of the strengths in my business offset his business's weaknesses. And vice versa. There were certainly synergies to be had, and we would double our executive oversight of the business with a merger.

We had our lawyers draw up the appropriate paperwork. We had a lot to consider. A merger of two companies is analogous to getting married. We were combining not only the two companies that we built ourselves from scratch, but we were also combining our finances, opportunities, and futures.

We had to hammer out how we'd work together, who held what amount of equity in the new company, and what each of our roles would be. It required many conversations and much planning. The agreement needed to document all of these things. Once drafted, we took a few weeks to read through it and make sure we wanted to proceed. Once we made up our minds, we proceeded quickly.

Erik Olson on the left, Kevin Daisey on the right, after signing the merger paperwork at our lawyer's office.

We signed the paperwork on a Monday afternoon. The next day, we rented a U-Haul and moved both of our companies out of their old offices and into a new, much larger office. Once moved in, we started the process of settling in as a new, combined company.

After merging, our annual revenue that year was technically $1.2 million when you combined the $900K I had earned and the $300K he had earned. After eight years of struggling, I had finally exceeded $1 million/year. We had finally made it out of the 96 percent of businesses that linger below $1 million in revenue forever, or die trying.

Although we were technically a million dollar company, we had only done that by combining our independently earned revenue. It was a milestone, but it didn't feel quite as good as I had hoped for. I wouldn't be happy until together, as the new company, we earned $1 million.

The merger was one of the most significant pivots I had made to date. In the past, I had pivoted from a career in civil engineering to software development, and from being an employee to an employer. But with this pivot I had the most at risk. I had joined forces with someone I'd only known for a few months. Would it work out? Would I even like working with Kevin? Luckily, our styles complemented each other and we got along great.

After all, we're similar and both share a vision of growing big. Once we got past the turbulence of merging our companies, our staff, and our cultures, we needed to put effort into what exactly this new company would focus on.

→ A new valley of death

Going into the merger, our plan was to build sophisticated applications that not only worked great, but also looked great and were amazing to use. Throughout 2017, we executed on that plan, adding branding and marketing pizzazz to what we built. Each application was also complemented with a snazzy marketing website that properly sold the product to potential customers.

With the increased workload of our combined companies, we hired a few more people. We also decided to add digital marketing as a service. Our thought process was that after we built a website or mobile app for a client, we could continue to service them with digital marketing. After all, our clients needed continued marketing support after we delivered what they hired us to build. Kevin and I had both dabbled in digital marketing, but it wasn't our forte, so we hired Jake to be a one-man digital marketing show for our clients.

As projects came and went, clients always needed marketing afterward. Although the big money was in software development, there was a long-tail aspect of marketing that I didn't appreciate much at first.

We had a tremendous number of software development leads in the summer of 2017. That was good because we had a whole crew of expensive software developers who we needed to put to work. At one point, we seriously discussed options for acquiring more office space because we were about to get slammed with so much work. We had four or five new big projects teed up by early fall. We just needed one or two of them to come through, and we were going to kill it!

Summer turned into autumn, and before we knew it, Thanksgiving had passed. Frustratingly for us, our "sure thing" leads stopped returning our calls. We pressed on and kept trying to close them. When we were lucky enough to speak with them, they'd tell us they still wanted to work with us but needed more time. As Thanksgiving transitioned into Christmas, we realized we were getting ghosted. We were unlikely to land any of these "sure things."

We also realized that our existing projects were coming to an end. By definition, a project has a start date and an end date. All projects end. At that time, Christmas 2017, about one-third of our projects had already ended, and another one-third would wrap up in a couple of weeks. We were running out of work.

If those leads didn't materialize, and with our existing work ramping down quickly, we recognized that we could find ourselves in trouble. If we didn't find new work quickly, we wouldn't expand. We'd be contracting.

Over the holidays, between Christmas and New Year's, the business world pretty much comes to a standstill. During downtime that week, I took a deep dive into our finances. I looked at our expenses and compared them to projections for which projects we could end up winning. But the prognosis was not good since most of our prospects had ghosted us for months.

What made me think they'd all of a sudden come around after dodging us for the entire fall and holiday season? What would it mean if none of those projects came to fruition?

I projected our revenue for the next year. At the least, I wanted to make what we had made the previous year. We had already booked about $200K in new work going into the new year. In order to just tread water, we'd have to find, sell, service, and collect another $1 million in work.

It was heartbreaking. Here we were currently operating at $1.2 million in revenue, but we only had $200K in revenue projected so far for 2018. We had a huge gap in our finances. Kevin and I were going to have to hustle hard to fill a million dollar gap, or our company would shrink.

Not happy with my revenue projection, I next broke down our expenses into the different services we offered. Our expenses were classified as software development, marketing websites, website support, or digital marketing. Once I understood how much we spent on expenses supporting each of those services, I projected how much revenue we had already secured for each service going into 2018.

Again, the outlook was not great. In aggregate, the projections at the service level added up to the same as the company projections. But I noticed a few differences this time.

First, the bulk of the $1M revenue gap at the company level came from software development. Although it was the most profitable for us, it was also the hardest to secure. Turns out we'd have to collect a whopping $700K in new projects just to match our 2017 revenue in that category! That's a lot of new work to find, complete, and get paid for, and we didn't have any good leads at the moment.

Second, our marketing websites and website support services were also projected to be in the red. We'd have to find another $300K in new projects in these two categories just to break even in 2018.

But there was one silver lining.

Although small, our digital marketing service was projected to be profitable. We only had a handful of digital marketing clients. That meant there wasn't a ton of revenue, but our expenses were low. Digital marketing was making a profit, but since revenue was relatively low, it didn't amount to much profit.

But what digital marketing offered that the other services didn't was continual work. Unlike project work, digital marketing doesn't have an end date. It's not so much a project as a continuing campaign. Marketing never ends; it just changes over time. Clients always need marketing and our digital marketing services would recur into the foreseeable future.

→ Focusing on our future

Since marketing was a recurring activity, the likelihood was high that those clients, and that revenue, would stay with the company until at least the end of the year. We had contracts that provided for monthly payments and recurring revenue. As long as we kept providing our clients with digital marketing services that they valued, they'd stay with us. Although the profits from digital marketing didn't add up to much money, the profit margin was healthy.

With the healthy profit margin, selling more digital marketing would amount to more dollars. If we got more of that kind of work, the profit in dollars would start to increase.

With that realization, we started on the next phase of our company's history. Our plan was simple: get more digital marketing work, which meant recurring revenue.

Though simple, the plan was fraught with risk. It's not every day that you completely shift the focus of your company from one type of work to another. Many bad things could happen along the way. If the timing on our transition was not just right, then we could lose developers before they finished the work they had started. Or, if we kept developers on for too long, then we could blow through our cash reserves and not live to see another day. At the same time, we also had to hire and train new digital marketers as we transitioned from the software business.

Project revenue would be replaced by recurring revenue, which would bring a slew of issues along with it. We had to update contracts, rework terms and conditions, and rethink every workflow process. We were built for project work and our systems had to be re-engineered for recurring revenue.

Everything was changing, and all at once. We felt like we had no time to spare, and we hurried with the transition. Such rapid change, in such a compressed time frame, is risky. Everything could go horribly wrong. But we realized and agreed that our greatest risk was to do nothing. If we hoped for the best, and hoped that the software business would magically turn back around, we could lose everything we'd worked for over the past decade.

We just wouldn't let that happen. No matter the struggle, we were going to brute-force transition Array Digital into a digital marketing powerhouse.

Like most years before it, 2018 was a year of struggle to find our purpose and a more stable business model. But little by little, we got more digital marketing work. Soon we hired another digital marketer. As our software department continued to limp along, our digital marketing department was growing. The plan appeared to be working. Slower than I had hoped for, but it was coming together, nonetheless.

Our pursuit of getting more digital marketing would eventually change the direction of our company. A pivot was coming, a significant pivot, to completely focus the company on digital marketing and recurring revenue.

Although we were in the throes of transitioning from project revenue to recurring revenue, and transitioning from a software development company to a digital marketing agency, we maintained our revenue levels at just north of $1 million/year in 2018. It was close, but we were still part of the 4 percent club of companies that earned $1 million per year in revenue.

By the end of 2018, the transition was complete. We had wrapped up the bulk of our software projects, our software developers had moved on to other companies, and we had staffed up with digital marketers. With the transition, and a makeover of our marketing message to focus exclusively on digital marketing, our revenues began to climb.

Not only did our revenue climb, but it climbed consistently and predictably. Our revenue source was stable and growing and continues to grow to this day. Remember in the beginning of *Million Dollar Journey* where I wrote that your first million will be your toughest? It was, and by a long shot. It took me eight long years, with many missteps, to reach one million dollars in revenue. Once we crossed that threshold, our revenue never decreased. In fact, it's increasing at its fastest rate yet.

With fixed expenses and an expanding portfolio of clients, it became easy for us to project our finances and growth into the future. The recurring revenue that came with digital marketing meant we no longer had to find and deliver millions of dollars of new project work every year, year after year.

Recurring revenue meant we could stop incessantly chasing the dollar. Instead we could land clients and focus on providing great services and results. If we got more clients, great. But unlike before, if we didn't land new clients, then we weren't at risk of going out of business.

No longer did new clients replace old clients. New clients were in addition to old clients.

I could finally see a path forward for the company. I could finally begin to imagine where all this could go.

→ When to pivot

Our pivot to digital marketing was a massive transition for us. But it wasn't the first transition I've made.

I had transitioned from civil engineering to software development and later to digital marketing. I had transitioned from working for companies to owning a company. Transition, it seems, is a natural state for me.

Many entrepreneurs I know are uncomfortable with transitioning. Although they see the signs on the wall, signs telling them they should consider pivoting their business, many simply ignore them.

If you find yourself in a similar situation, ask yourself which future you'd prefer ... one where you continue to have the same struggles you're having now, or one where your current struggles are behind you and you're moving onward?

It's easy to get paralyzed into inaction. Pivoting is hard. It's not natural, and it's not straightforward. You won't know if you're doing the right thing until after you've started down your new path.

But if you see your company on a downward spiral, don't ride your current situation down to zero. Before you crash and burn, you'll have a window of opportunity to pivot. Evaluate if the window is narrow or wide—that will tell you how fast you need to pivot.

Or, you may decide to not pivot. It's clearly your choice and yours alone. But which is going to get you to the seven-figure mark? Remember, your goal is not simply to earn a living. It's to excel and to create a million dollar company. If pivoting away from your comfort zone is the way to do it, then you'll need to do it.

Chapter takeaways

1. If your company lacks a service that would make you more whole, seek out another company that you can partner with to fill the gap.
2. Once you find a good company to partner with, test them out. Work on multiple projects together.
3. A merger or acquisition can be used to permanently fill your service gaps. When considering a merger or acquisition, take time to consider the pros and cons of what you're about to do and how it will affect your key employees and yourself.
4. There will be a period of time after a merger or acquisition when you have to come to terms with what you just did. Combining companies is a merging of power, authority, resources, personnel, and processes. The coming together won't happen overnight. Be patient, but hurry on with it.
5. You'll likely end up pivoting more than once. Always be on the lookout for signs that a pivot may be needed. Don't ignore the signs. Always ask if a pivot will improve your position as a company and if it will help you get to where you want to go.

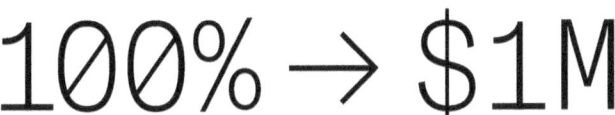

100% → $1M

 14

The journey to
$100 million

My painted picture from the first chapter is of a scene that happens a long time from today. Your painted picture will likely look different than mine. If you haven't started on your entrepreneurial journey yet, then it may be near impossible to imagine what your painted picture could look like.

Although my painted picture won't come to fruition until 2030, in reality, it's taken me over twenty-five years of hard work to get to the point of being able to see a future beyond my next paycheck. Yours won't happen overnight either.

After struggling in jobs that weren't a fit for my ambition, and after trying freelancing on and off for many years, an event beyond my control was the final kick in the ass I needed to get me moving in the right direction. But once going, and once in full control of my destiny, I started to envision a better future at work and at home.

A period of magical transformation began once I crossed the $1 million/year mark. With that milestone behind me, I was qualified to join other entrepreneurs in the Entrepreneurs' Organization. A global organization with local chapters, EO is filled with ambitious entrepreneurs who all want the best out of their lives.

My local chapter holds learning events, as well as all-day learning retreats every three months. At one of these quarterly learning retreats, the facilitator asked what our biggest goal was. A goal so big that any other achievement we accomplished during the next decade or so just wouldn't compare to it. He encouraged us to think big. Really big. What was the one thing we wanted most out of our professional lives?

Kevin, Jake, and I attended that session together. When we broke into small groups to discuss the goal we wanted to achieve, the three of us huddled off to the side of everyone else. We had ideas of what our success looked like, but it was hard to quantify.

Would it be the number of employees in the company? If so, how many? A thousand? Two thousand? It was hard to wrap our heads around what that really meant. Maybe the number should be how many offices we had. But that, too, was debatable because we also couldn't wrap our heads around it. Did that even make sense? What if we didn't need all those people and offices to achieve our goal? Maybe people and offices weren't the goal, but instead the means to an end.

I had a notion that revenue, a topic we understood well, was a way for us to quantify success. As discussed in Chapter 12 on goal-setting,

I knew we could achieve a tremendous amount over a decade or more. How much more revenue could we grow?

I could easily envision us as a $10 million or $20 million company. But recognizing the compound effect of small improvements maintained over time, and not wanting to set a goal too small, I knew those numbers were achievable.

What would be a stretch? A big stretch? Something so big that people may think we're crazy? What amount of revenue above $20 million should we shoot for?

As we debated, I realized I already had a number in mind, but I was afraid to say the words. "One hundred million dollars," I blurted out. I wouldn't be satisfied until we grew to be a $100 million company.

It was a significantly high goal considering where we were, at the time just barely over $1 million/year. Shoot, we barely qualified for EO at the time. It was almost a rounding error that our revenue was over the $1 million/year minimum! How could we possibly think we'd grow by one hundred times?

It seemed appalling to pick a goal of $100 million. Ridiculously ambitious. But that's just what we decided we'd achieve over the next decade. By setting a goal so high, it forced us to pause and ask, How could we possibly accomplish that?

We'd picked a big number, for sure. Now I had to figure out what that meant in terms of growth. Was it even possible to grow that much in such a relatively short amount of time? Could we grow the way I wanted to, with recurring revenue?

Success, like interest in an investment account, compounds over time. Success stacks upon itself.

I ran a bunch of calculations. We were growing our recurring revenue by an astounding 250 percent year over year. Here's what it would look like if that growth rate continued.

Growth Rate	250%
Years	**ARR**
1	$1,100,000
2	$3,850,000
3	$13,475,000
4	$47,162,500
5	$165,068,750

So it'd take us only five years to get to $100 million at that rate. Seems crazy ... was that right? Could we actually continue to grow at 250 percent for five years straight? Without outside funding, it seemed extremely unlikely.

What if the growth rate was more reasonable at 100 percent per year? How long would it take if we doubled our revenue every year? I ran that calculation too.

Growth Rate	100%
Years	ARR
1	$1,100,000
2	$2,200,000
3	$4,400,000
4	$8,800,000
5	$17,600,000
6	$35,200,000
7	$70,400,000
8	$140,800,000

If we lowered our expectations from our current growth rate of 250 percent to 100 percent, then we'd reach $100 million in eight years. But even a 100 percent growth rate seemed extremely aggressive. What if an economic downturn hit us? Would we be able to average 100 percent growth year over year consistently?

As confident as I was in our business model, I doubted we would maintain 100 percent growth rates every year without fail.

How about asking the question a different way? What if we picked a year that we wanted to hit the goal by and then calculated what percentage of growth would be required to reach $100 million by that date? It was late 2018 when I made this calculation. Ten years out was 2028.

We decided to round up to 2030, a moderately long time away, and a nice round number. Seemed legitimate enough to us, and we ran with 2030. Twelve full years were in between, including 2019 and 2030 (we gave ourselves to the end of 2030 to reach the goal).

Then the question was, *What growth rate would be required to reach $100 million in twelve years?* Going back to the spreadsheet, I reworked the formulas and came up with ...

Growth Rate	55%
Years	**ARR**
01	$1,100,000
02	$1,705,000
03	$2,642,750
04	$4,096,263
05	$6,349,207
06	$9,841,271
07	$15,253,970
08	$23,643,653
09	$36,647,662
10	$56,803,876
11	$88,046,007
12	$136,471,311

To reach our goal of growing from our present $1.1 million in annual recurring revenue to $100 million in annual recurring revenue, our recurring revenue would need to increase by about 55 percent annually on average.

Was that reasonable? I could foresee years of stagnant growth, or even negative growth, if and when a recession hit. But I could also see growth spurts happening where our growth rate could be significantly higher than 55 percent.

In the end, we liked it. A growth rate of 55 percent seemed not only reasonable, but likely. We felt we could accomplish this ridiculously audacious goal, especially with the support, guidance, and ideas of our Array Mentors mastermind group.

Now, it's your turn.

Set a goal to join the 4 percent of businesses that reach $1 million in revenue. Follow the processes laid out in *Million Dollar Journey*. Consider the path I took and what you can learn from my successes and especially from my failures.

What can you apply from this book to build your own seven-figure business? I bet you can do it even faster than I did. I'm cheering for you.

Go build the future you want!

→ MILLION DOLLAR JOURNEY

→

About the author

ABOUT THE AUTHOR

Erik J. Olson is the Founder and CEO of Array Digital—a digital marketing agency headquartered in Chesapeake, Virginia. Find more information about Array Digital at thisisarray.com. Erik is also the host of the Journey to $100 Million, a daily podcast and Amazon flash briefing. Listen to the podcast at journeyto100million.com.

Erik often speaks on the topics of entrepreneurship and digital marketing. Happily married for over twenty years, and with two beautiful daughters, Erik enjoys spending his free time training for triathlons, weight lifting, and relaxing outdoors.

Find Erik online at iamerikjolson.com, follow him on social media everywhere at @iamerikjolson, and check out his premier business mastermind at arraymentors.com.

Array Mentors

Most of us are on a journey by ourselves. Without a compass or map, we stumble along the best we can.

How much more successful would you be if you could harness the experiences of a group of successful business owners?

What if you could learn from their successes and avoid mistakes they've made in the past? What if you could tap into business owners who you could turn to for advice and suggestions, and who could help solve your most pressing problems?

Array Mentors, my premier business mastermind, provides the framework and the guidance to help you find your way, get you on the right path, and accelerate your journey to success.

By joining Array Mentors, you'll surround yourself with like-minded business owners who understand intimately what you're going through on a daily basis.

It took us eight long years to go from freelancing to breaking through the $1 million per year mark. Only 4 percent of businesses break $1M in annual sales. That means that 96 percent of companies die trying, or linger in purgatory forever.

Yes, you could do it the hard way—never learn from others and simply plow through life making classic mistakes.

But it could take years, maybe decades, before you achieve even a modicum of your ambitions.

What we've found along our journey is that the best way to grow your business is ...

1. To work in your business full time. If you're still wondering how to make the leap from part time to full time, we'll get you there.
2. Learn from others who are ahead of you on the entrepreneurial journey.
3. Work on your business. Get out of the day-to-day and instead work on improving your processes and systems, making a better experience for your employees and clients.
4. Teach others what you've learned along the way (the best way to learn is to teach).

→ Is this mastermind right for you?

This mastermind is not for people who like to play entrepreneur on social media. We're looking for people who are launching or running real businesses.
If you ...

- → Already have a part-time or full-time business,
- → Made between $50K and $1M in the last twelve months, and
- → Want to aggressively grow your business ...
- → Then this may be the right mastermind for you.

→ It's not for everyone

We're not interested in loading up on members for the sake of growing the membership. We're looking for people who are just as dedicated to business as we are.

If you're not serious about going full time in your business in the next three to six months, then this is not for you. If you're looking to run a slow and steady lifestyle business, then this isn't for you. If you're near retirement and want to cruise to the finish line, then this is not for you.

In order to get into this mastermind, you must want to grow your business, be transparent with the other mastermind members, and share your experiences with others.

You give to the membership, and they give back. Above all, you will be giving just as much as you are receiving.

→ Take the next step in your journey

For more information on Array Mentors, visit arraymentors.com.

You'll find answers to all your questions about this premier business mastermind. We invite you to join us!

Business Growth Mastermind

Goals

Goals

Goals

Goals

Take notes

ACKNOWLEDGMENTS

I would like to thank several people for their contributions to *Million Dollar Journey*. First to my wife, Lia, who has always encouraged me to fulfill my dreams.

Thanks to my Array Digital co-founder, Kevin Daisey, for trusting in me. Joining forces was one of the best business decisions I've ever made. Thank you as well to every employee who has entrusted their livelihood and career with me, as well as to all of our clients.

Thanks to previous business partners who have taught me so much along the way, often and unfortunately at their expense, as I learned through every failure; my wife, Lia, as partners in LaChoclatier Bakery, and to Clinton Stevens as partners at Syntactical.

Thanks to those who have supported and shaped me into the person that I am today. To you, my original mentors and role models, my parents Larry and Janet Olson, thank you. Thanks to previous bosses who coped with me as I found my way from employee to entrepreneur; my father Larry Olson, Bill Sweetser, Jack Waschitz, John Hartung, Rod Davis, Mark Morrison, and Chris Wollerman. To the Entrepreneurs' Organization, especially to members of the Southeast Virginia chapter, and to my forum mates in Forum 6. To trusted advisors Zack Miller, Danijel Velicki, Gabe McCoy, Owen Van Syckle, Brad Hunter, and to Jason Swenk and all the members of his mastermind.

Finally, thank you to those who have had a hand in bringing this book into reality. To Zack Miller for encouraging me to start the *Journey to $100 Million* podcast and to write *Million Dollar Journey*. To my wife, Lia, for being understanding when I isolated myself for hours at a time to write. Thank you to Jennifer Jas for editing this manuscript, and to my cousin and art director, Scott Massey, for an amazing cover!

Acknowledgments

→